A

CALL

TO

HOLINESS

Second Printing

**by
Bruce R. Booker, Ph.D.**

Copyright 1994
by
Bruce R. Booker, Ph.D.
Printed in the United States of America
Second Printing - 2003

ISBN: 0-9660041-0-8
Library of Congress Catalog Card Number: 97-094237

The pictures found in Chapter 3 are taken from the Israel Corel Professional Photos CD-ROM, Copyright 1993 by Corel Corporation.

The drawing in Chapter 5 was created by Daniel Botkin.

After these things, I saw another angel coming down from
heaven. He had great authority, the earth was lit up by his
splendor. He cried out in a strong voice,
"She has fallen! She has fallen!
Bavel the Great!
She has become a home for demons, prison for every
unclean spirit, prison for every unclean, hated bird.
"For all the nations have drunk of the wine of God's fury
caused by her whoring - yes, the kings of the earth went
whoring with her, and from her unrestrained love of
luxury the world's businessmen have grown rich." Then I
heard another voice out of heaven say:
"My people, come out of her!
So that you will not share in her sins, so that you
will not be infected by her plagues, for her sins
are a sticky mess piled up to heaven, and
God has remembered her crimes."

REVELATION 18:1-5

CONTENTS

PREFACE

The Basis: A Holy People

God wants a holy people.

There is a revival on the horizon; many can feel it; many have preached it. Yet, though we all desire revival, I am convinced that we believers are perhaps the very reason why it is not occurring in the Body of Messiah today.

I believe that the reason why there is no sweeping trans-denominational revival in the Body of Messiah today is because we have little desire to be a holy people — as God has defined holy. Yet, God wants His people to be a holy people, and when Yeshua comes back, he wants to come back to a Body made clean and ready (Revelation 19:7) - to a believing community who has put away the filth of the world system.

The object of this book is not to stand in condemnation of the Body of Messiah universal, that is the true believers from every denomination since, **Therefore, there is no longer any condemnation awaiting those who are in union with the Messiah Yeshua.** (Romans 8:1).

Through this message I do not say that believers who practice unscriptural things are condemned by God, rather, that true believers who practice these things need to take Biblical reproof and cease such practices.

All Scripture is God-breathed and is valuable for teaching the truth, convicting of sin, correcting faults and training in right living; thus anyone who belongs to God may be fully equipped for every good work. (2 Timothy 3:16,17).

It must be stressed that Scriptural reproof and correction is not condemnation! When a loving father reproves his children, he does not condemn them nor disown them. He disciplines them and though the chastening for the present does not feel good, it yields the peaceable fruit of righteousness unto those who are exercised by this discipline (Hebrews 12:7-11).

Many will perhaps feel threatened by what I write in this book for it goes against what they have been taught all their lives. Yet, if it accomplishes the intended purposes in the heart of the believer who truly loves Yeshua and desires to serve Him, then this labor of love has been worth it. This purpose is to draw the hearts of men, women, boys and girls back to God and the simplicity and purity of His Word, for them to walk as Messiah walked (1 John 2:3-6).

A follower of Messiah should want to follow Messiah in all ways, not just the paths that he or she likes, but even unto death, especially death to self. To do this we have to put aside pride and selfrighteousness and admit our errors and the errors of our people, even as Daniel did:

I prayed to Adonai my God and made this confession:

"Please Adonai, great and fearsome God, who keeps his covenant and extends grave to those who love him and observe his mitzvot! We have sinned, done wrong, acted wickedly, rebelled and turned away from your mitzvot and rulings." (Daniel 9:4,5).

It is when we do this that God will restore to us the place wherewith He has called us a holy people of God.

Acknowledgments

First and foremost I wish to express my gratitude to God and His unfailing mercy and love who gave me the strength to write this book. It is He who made it clear to me that grace and Law work hand-in-hand and are not in mutual opposition the one to the other. He also showed me that to truly love Him, we need to keep His commandments.

Secondly, I wish to thank my wife Pat who had to persevere with me as I dedicated my time and energies to this book.

Furthermore, I am grateful to Diane McNeal and Donna Sularin who edited this book and offered suggestions to make it more receivable by the brethren in the body of Messiah.

Finally, I would like to express my sincere gratitude to Dale and Loretta Jacobs for making this second printing possible.

Chapter 1

What is Holiness?

In God's Word we find Him commanding us to be a "holy" people. Yet, with so many "holy" things in this world, how are we to know what "holiness" truly is?

There are many things deemed to be holy: "holy water," "holy garments," "holy war," "holy communion," "holy sacraments," "holy priesthood," "holy animals," "holy matrimony," "holy sacrifices," "holy men," "holy women," "holy, holy, holy" — Holy mackerel! How are we to know what truly is Biblically "holy"?

In Hebrew the word for "holy" is kadosh which, according to Gesenius' Hebrew-Chaldee Lexicons to the Old Testament means **"pure, clean, free from defilement of crimes, idolatry, and other unclean and profane things."**[1] In the Greek New Testament "hagiasmos" is rendered as **"sanctification," signifying a "separation to God, and the resultant state or conduct befitting those so separated."**[2]

It stands to reason that since the Bible is a Hebrew book, we need to understand what holiness is from its Hebrew background and not from our definition. Holiness is not simply a title but an attitude of the heart reflected in how we live our lives. Holiness is defined within the Torah, providing the framework upon which all the other Books of the Bible depend.

The other fundamental thought of the Book [of Leviticus] is Holiness, i.e. purity of life, purity of action, purity of

---

1   *Gesenius 'Hebrew-Chaldee Lexicon to the Old Testament*, H.W.F. Gesenius, BAKER BOOK HOUSE, Grand Rapids, MI, Copyright 1979, page 722.

2   *Vine's Expository Dictionary of Biblical Words*, W.E. Vine, THOMAS NELSON PUBLISHERS, New York, Copyright 1985, page 307.

thought, befitting a priestly Nation. All the precepts in Leviticus are merely a translation into terms of daily life of the Divine call, "Ye shall be holy; for I the Lord your God am holy" (xix, 2). Holiness is an active principle, shaping and regulating every sphere of human life and activity. In Chap. Xix, the demand, "Ye shall be holy," is included in a series of sublime ethical doctrines; in Chap. Xi, it is embodied in the dietary laws. The rule of Holiness governs the body as well as the soul, since the body is the instrument through which alone the soul acts. The Holy People of the Holy God was to keep itself free not only from moral transgressions, but also from ceremonial defilement, which would weaken the barriers against the forces of heathenism and animalism that on all sides menaced Israel.[3]

Holiness is not only a separation of ourselves unto God as His own personal possession, but also a separation of ourselves from the worldly ways.

In an ethical sense holiness signifies the attainment of moral purity and perfection through right conduct and especially by imitating the Divine attributes. Essentially holiness is an attribute of God, who alone is "holy with every form of holiness" (Y. Ber. 9a) , and the most common epithet for God in rabbinical literature is "The Holy One, blessed be He."

Man attains holiness to the extent that he consciously models his life and conduct upon the known attributes of God. "As He is merciful, be thou merciful; as He is gracious, be thou gracious" (Shabbat 133b). Originally, however, holiness was not an ethical term: the basic concept is rather one of "separateness," the Divine attribute of being apart from that which is not Divine. As a result of the covenant of God, Israel too became "separate" and accepted a state of holiness which was to inform henceforth all its activities and even have physical implications. Israel is separated as

---

3   *The PENTATEUCH AND HAFTORAHS*, Second Edition, Edited by J.H. Hertz, Copyright 1987 by Soncino Press, page 409

a 'holy people' the priests and Levites are separated as a holy caste responsible for Temple ritual; the Sabbath is separated as a holy day; the Temple itself is separated as the place where man could worship the Divine Presence in the Holy of Holies...

Nevertheless the "separation" implicit in holiness is by no means to be regarded as a withdrawal from the world and its temptations, and Judaism has always opposed reclusion and extreme asceticism. It insists on the attainment of holiness by remaining separate from contaminating things while still living in their presence.[4]

The Hebrew concept of holiness is not that of withdrawal from the world but that of living in the world, yet remaining unstained by its contamination. Yet, many of the Laws found in Torah have an effect of separating God's people from their unbelieving neighbors.

For instance, the Biblical Laws of kashruit (kosher- "clean") with regard to things eaten (or not to be eaten) not only prevented defilement of God's people, but also had the effect of separating them from having table relations with the heathens surrounding them. To the Hebrew mind, eating with someone means that you are at peace with them. Essentially, you don't have someone at the table with you unless you are at peace with them, because it is at the table that you should be able to relax and let your guard down.

The truth is once you begin to have table relations with someone, you begin to build up a relationship with that person. You begin to accept them, to share ideas with them and ultimately, should your daughters or sons begin to build up a relationship with their daughters and sons, you intermarry with them and you or your children become like them.

---

4   *THE ENCYCLOPEDIA OF THE JEWISH RELIGION*, Edited by Dr. R.J. Zwi Werblowsky and Dr. Geoffrey Wigoder, Copyright 1986 by ADAMA BOOKS, pages 188-189.

This is what God was trying to prevent:

Adonai your God is going to bring you into the land you will enter in order to take possession of it, and he will expel many nations ahead of you - the Hitti, Girgashi, Emori, Kena'ani, P'rizi, Hivi and Y'vusi, seven nations bigger and stronger than you. When he does this, when Adonai your God hands them over ahead of you, and you defeat them, you are to destroy them completely! Do not make any covenant with them. Show them no mercy. Don't intermarry with them - don't give your daughter to his son, and don't take his daughter for your son. For he will turn your children away from following me in order to serve other gods. If this happens, the anger of Adonai will flare up against you, and he will quickly destroy you. No, treat them this way: break down their altars, smash their standing-stones to pieces, cut down their sacred poles and burn up their carved images completely. For you are a people set apart as holy for Adonai your God. Adonai your God has chosen you out of all the peoples on the face of the earth to be his own unique treasure. (Deuteronomy 7:1-6)

The reason for this separation from ungodly people was so that God's holy people would not begin to practice the wickedness that those people practiced. In brief, if you don't eat with them and fellowship with them, then it is less likely that you will build relationships with them. If you don't build relationships with them, you will be less likely to like them, learn their practices and ultimately become as they are.

Clearly, the kashruit laws prevented the Hebrew people from having table relations with the ungodly people surrounding them, since those nations often ate things God's people were forbidden to eat. A degree of discomfort, no doubt, existed when a Hebrew would be invited to a dinner of ham only to turn down the one inviting him because he was not allowed to eat the meat. Or when a Hebrew would invite someone over to their house for dinner and they bring something over that is unkosher for dessert, such as "blood pudding."

In human society, our "food" is near and dear to our heart. In many cultures, to refuse to eat something is tantamount to a major offense! Sharing food is part of relationship-building and contributes to a healthy friendship.

Since my wife and I observe a Biblical kashruit, we are careful to bring to the table only what is biblically kosher. Likewise, when we eat at someone's house, we will only eat what is Biblically kosher. When we are invited to people's houses who don't share the same convictions, we are always on our guard to insure that we are not eating something unkosher. If they ask us ahead of time what we like, we try to steer them toward Biblical kosher without making a big deal of it. On the other hand, if we aren't given the opportunity of being asked what we like and are at the dinner table with them, we quietly dish up only what we recognize to be free from treif (unkosher things).

I realize that some believers would say that we should eat anything set before us since 1 Corinthians 10:27 says:

If some unbeliever invites you to eat a meal, and you want to go, eat whatever is put in front of you without raising questions of conscience.

I disagree with their interpretation of this passage. If we look at the context of this passage, we will see that the issue deals with eating meat that may, or may not, have been sacrificed to idols, since in the meat market at that time no one could be sure whether that meat was sacrificed to idols or not.

The issue here is not whether the meat set before them was kosher or not (I'll deal with that subject in a later chapter), it is whether the meat about to be eaten by them was sacrificed to an idol. Shaul (the Apostle Paul) here isn't saying, "Go ahead, eat the meat offered to idols" or he would have been violating the Acts 15:20 and 29 injunction. What he is saying here is: "Don't ask."

Now, back to our subject of table relations. My wife and I find that our deepest friendships are built with people who share the same perspectives on this matter, since we don't have to keep our guard up about what we are eating and we can focus on building relationship. For some reason, we don't seem to achieve the same degree of depth with those whom we have to keep our guard up. It seems therefore, because of the kosher laws, we have a form of separation to keep us from having that type of relationship.

God placed this form of separation and other forms in His Law to protect His people from becoming like the world surrounding them. It was good that He did this. If He didn't, there would not be a distinct group of people through whom the Messiah ultimately would come. The Hebrew people would have assimilated with the other nations and would have been no more.

God still has these forms of separation for His people today or we, too, would assimilate into the world and be no longer a distinct people.

As people who obey God, do not let yourselves be shaped by the evil desires you used to have when you were still ignorant. On the contrary, following the Holy One who called you, become holy yourselves in your entire way of life; since the Tanakh says, "You are to be holy because I am holy." (1 Peter 1:14-16)

Peter gets this quote from Leviticus 11:45. He is saying here that we, as believers, are to imitate God.

Man is not only to worship God, but to imitate Him. By his deeds he must reveal the Divine that is implanted in him; and make manifest, by the purity and righteousness of his actions that he is of God. Mortal man cannot imitate God's infinite majesty or His eternity; but he can strive towards a

purity that is Divine, by keeping aloof from everything loath-
some and defiling (xi, 44); and especially can he imitate
God's merciful qualities. This "imitation of God" is held
forth by the Rabbis as the highest human ideal...

Holiness is thus not so much an abstract or a mystic idea, as
a regulative principle in the everyday lives of men and
women. The words "ye shall be holy," are the keynote of
the whole chapter, and must be read in connection with its
various precepts; reverence for parents, consideration for
the needy, prompt wages for reasonable hours, honourable
dealing, no talebearing or malice, love of one's neighbour
and cordiality to the alien, equal justice to rich and poor,
just measures and balances - together with abhorrence of
everything unclean, irrational, or heathen. Holiness is thus
not attained by flight from the world, nor by monk-like renunciation of human relationships of family or station, but
by the spirit in which we fulfil the obligations of life in its
simplest and commonest details: in this way - by doing justly,
loving mercy, and walking humbly with our God - is everyday life transfigured.[5]

Literally, God is saying, "Be separate from the world, for I am
separate from the world." Holiness is separateness from the
world and it's lusts. True holiness is being in the world, but not
having friendship with the world system which is based on self-
ishness and greed.

1 John 2:15-17 says:

Do not love the world or the things of the world. If someone
loves the world, then love for the Father is not in him; because all the things of the world - the desires of the old nature, the desires of the eyes, and the pretensions of life - are
not from the Father but from the world. And the world is

5   *The PENTATEUCH AND HAFTORAHS*, Second Edition, Edited by J.H. Hertz,
Copyright 1987 by Soncino Press, page 497-498

passing away, along with its desires. But whoever does God's will remains forever.

You unfaithful wives! Don't you know that loving the world is hating God? Whoever chooses to be the world's friend makes himself God's enemy! (James 4:4)

Sadly, many believers attempt to walk a razor thin line - trying to be friends with the world and with God. They compromise what they know to be true from the Word of God and act like the world.

They are living in the world much as Lot was living in Sodom. Now, Lot didn't start out living in Sodom, he set his tents just outside the city (Genesis 13:12). However, the next time we see him in Scripture, he is living in the city (Genesis 14:12). You would think that this was bad enough, but when we see his name again, we see him sitting in the gates of the city (Genesis 19:1). This means that he was regarded an elder or judge of the city, for it was in the gates that the elders would sit to judge between individuals coming to them for justice. Lot was no longer a visitor or stranger in Sodom, he was part of the citizenry!

Did the ungodliness of Sodom rub off on Lot and his family? Two passages indicated it had. The first, when the angels sent to rescue Lot and his family came, the men of the city wanted to have sexual relations with these angels. Lot does not simply say, "No way." But, instead, he offers his virgin daughters to these men to do with as they like. The second passage was after the rescue when Lot's daughters made their father drunk with wine and had sexual relations with him, producing offspring by their father.

From these passages, it is important to realize this: you can't walk in a pigpen without getting some of its filth on you. A believer who thinks they can walk in worldly ways without getting defiled is deceiving him or herself.

Yet, over the centuries, the Body of Messiah has incorporated within itself many of the worldly ways and has played the "harlot" to the nations. From the passage in Revelation 18:1-5 it is evident that some of God's people are found within this harlot Babylon, or God wouldn't have to call them out of her. This doesn't mean that the believers found within the harlot are Babylon, but rather that they are a part of this religious system and need to come out of her.

God has always warned His people against the religious practices of the nations – Exodus 23:24, 32- 33; 34:12; Deuteronomy 7:2-6; 25-26. Yet, the Jewish people often fell into the pagan practices of the nations surrounding them. When they did practice the religious observances of these nations, He likened her to a prostitute – Ezekiel 16, Hosea, etc.

God did not offer comforting, placating words for them so that they could continue their rebelliousness. Instead, in Jeremiah 2:20-3:10 we see a different word coming from God to His chosen people. Following are a few of these passages:

For long ago I broke your yoke; when I snapped your chains, you said, "I won't sin." Yet on every high hill, under every green tree, you sprawled and prostituted yourself.
(Verse 20)

How can you say, "I am not defiled, I have not pursued the ba'alim"? Look at your conduct in the valley, understand what you have done.
You are a restive young female camel, running here and there, wild, accustomed to the desert, sniffing the wind in her lust - who can control her when she's in heat?
Males seeking her need not weary themselves, for at mating season they will find her.
(Verses 23-24)

Adonai says, "If a man divorces his wife, and she leaves him and marries another man, then if the first one marries her again, that land will be completely defiled. But you prostituted yourself to many lovers, yet you want to return to me?" says Adonai.
(Chapter 3, verse 1)

If God spoke this way to His people Israel, whom He loved, why should He only speak sweet things to His Body (who should know better) when we have done the same thing.

As had occurred with Israel over the centuries, the Body of the Lord Yeshua haMashiach (Jesus, the Messiah) has incorporated into its religious observances the practices forbidden by God – the practices of the neighboring nations. As a result the Body is defiled and in need of cleansing, just as Israel was. Yet, in spite of what He said in Jeremiah, He still invites His people to repentance (Jeremiah 3:12-4:12).

Go and proclaim these words toward the north:

"Return, backsliding Isra'el," says Adonai. "I will not frown on you, for I am merciful," says Adonai. "I will not bear a grudge forever. Only acknowledge your guilt, that you have committed crimes against Adonai your God, that you were promiscuous with strangers under every green tree, and that you have not paid attention to my voice," says Adonai.
(Chapter 3, verses 12 and 13)

Let us lie down in our shame, let our disgrace cover us, for we have sinned against Adonai our God, both we and our ancestors, from our youth until today; we have not paid attention to the voice of Adonai our God. (Chapter 3 verse 25)

Just as God was inviting Israel to repent and put away her foreign gods and practices, so is He speaking to the believing community today. The passage cited earlier on page 3 (Revelation 18), speaks to every believer to look at their practice of faith and see if they are found within this "Babylonian religious system." It is incumbent upon every true believer who loves God to hear this call and remove himself or herself from the harlot, though it may be costly. If not, they, too, will be a participant in Babylon's sins and will receive of her plagues.

The time of the end is near, and more than ever the Bride of Messiah needs to **"make herself ready"** (Revelation 19:7) by once again embracing the holiness that God requires of her as found in His commandments, a holiness that is not in name, but in truth.

In reality, true holiness is not simply a title as some think but a state of being. God does not merely want us to be called "holy," but God wants us to be holy or separate from the world and how it operates. We are to pursue holiness as a people (Hebrews 12:14), for without that holiness, no one will see God. The question is, "How are we to be truly holy, to be what God wants us to be?"

Chapter 2

A Call to Holiness

Today's world is a relativistic world; moral relativism insists that there are no true, fixed standards of morality. "If it feels good [and it doesn't hurt someone, some add], do it," is the credo of this philosophy. On the other hand, God's world is a world of standards. He sets the standards of what is right and what is wrong, of what is holy and profane.

Sadly, when we look at the Body of Messiah today, we find it unsure of what constitutes holiness and what doesn't. Some Christian denominations have no problem with homosexuals marrying each other or holding leadership positions within its denomination. Some denominations have no problem with women being pastors or elders, teaching and leading men.

Some denominations place restrictions on behavior that is clearly super-scriptural or unscriptural: priests cannot marry, believers must not drink alcoholic beverages, smoke cigarettes, play cards, or go to a movie theater. They state dogmatically that such behavior is "against God's standards of holiness." Yet, when pressed to find the exact Scripture prohibiting that behavior, they cannot find it or often will infer it from a passage that is unrelated to the issue.

There is a sense in which the Body of Messiah itself has led the world to this morally-relative state, since it has wielded considerable power over the lives of millions of people through the centuries. This relativistic state comes about as a result of the prevailing "smorgasbord" mentality of the Body of Messiah.

For example, when the Body of Messiah approaches the Scriptures with this "smorgasbord" mentality, it states, in effect, that the Bible in its whole is not applicable to the lives of believers.

What tends to happen with this mind set is that people pick out those parts of the Bible they feel is still applicable and leave out the parts they feel are not. It is like going to a smorgasbord laden with an over abundance of food and you can take what you like and leave what you don't.

We hear preachers on Christian television and radio proclaiming the timely message, "We must keep God's commandments and follow God's standards of holiness," yet, when their theology is "pushed to the wall" (taken as far as it is possible to its logical conclusion) the standards they proclaim are far from God's.

For example, you hear few Christian preachers today proclaiming a return to God's Biblical standards of kashruit – kosher — (eating – what is to be eaten versus what isn't to be eaten). Yet, God is very clear in Leviticus 11 and Deuteronomy 14 about what may, and particularly what may not, be eaten, since it is pertinent to being holy as He is holy.

"Well," they reply, "we're no longer under the Law and don't have to follow the Mosaic laws of kashruit (smorgasbord mentality at work...)." They say that the Law is no longer valid as a standard of holiness in the life of a believer in Yeshua. Yet, it is definitely a standard of holiness in God's mind when He says:

For I am Adonai your God; therefore, consecrate yourselves and be holy, for I am holy; and do not defile yourselves with any kind of swarming creature that moves along the ground. (Maftir) For I am Adonai, who brought you up out of the land of Egypt to be your God. Therefore you are to be holy, because I am holy. (Leviticus 11: 44,45)

Considering that God does not change (Malachi 3:6; James 1:17; and Hebrews 13:8), it stands to reason that His holiness, or standards of holiness, do not change either! God still does not eat unkosher food (a little humor here), and neither should His believers.

On an aside; it is interesting to consider that the traditional Evangelical position relative to the Law is though the death of Yeshua fulfilled the penalty of the Law for all who placed their trust in Him, obedience to the Law of God is proof that one is a believer in Him. When we receive Him as Savior and Lord, the Law – the very same Law – is written in our hearts, not dispensed with.

In other words, the New Covenant simply takes the Law that God has already given and writes it upon the hearts and minds of the believers (Jeremiah 31:31-34; cf. Hebrews 8) so that we can keep it. It was given because people did not, in fact, could not, keep the Older covenant, a covenant external to them. Therefore, God created a new covenant, one written upon a heart of flesh and with a new Spirit (Ezekiel 36:26-27) so that people would be able to keep His Law:

I will give you a new heart and put a new spirit inside you; I will take the stony heart out of your flesh and give you a heart of flesh. I will put my Spirit inside you and cause you to live by my laws, respect my rulings and obey them.

If we look at Yeshua, we will see that He had just this type of heart and Spirit. He gave us the example we are to emulate: (1 John 2:3-6) if we walk by the Spirit, we will not carry out the desires of the flesh (i.e."sin") (Galatians 5). Yeshua kept the law perfectly; He always kept His Father's commandments. In order to be the propitiation for our sins (1 John 2:2) it was required that He fulfill the Law in absolute perfection. If the Church's assertion is true, that the keeping of the Law is "legalism" and those who keep the Law are "legalists," then, it logically follows that Yeshua was the perfect legalist, for He kept the Law perfectly!

Sorry folks, I don't think so. Yeshua gave us the example of how a Spirit-empowered believer *should act* without having to be provoked by a Law external to Himself to control His behavior (Luke 4:1, 14). The Law was *in* Him, (the essential element of the New Covenant proclaimed by Jeremiah 31:33), and was so much a part of Him (remember, this is God's nature) that He lived the Law naturally – without legalism! As Messiah Yeshua kept His Father's commandments and abode in His Father's love, so we, too, must keep His commandments and abide in His love. This is what it means to "know God."

I recall reading somewhere that Charles Finney once stated in a speech that the only difference between the Old Covenant and the New Covenant is that the New provides the power to do what the Old requires, but did not provide the power to do. He was "right on" with this position! If the Body of Messiah would embrace this understanding, we would not be far from the truth. May God again bring us quickly to this truth!

I'm not as concerned with the hows and whys of the world's current relativistic state; it has always been rebellious to God's standards. What concerns me most is how the Body of Messiah moved away from the holiness that God desires in all His people, not just the Jew, to its current position or relativism.

I believe that our current state is a result of a dispensationalist theology formulated by J.N. Darby in the early 1830's (though similar views were espoused by many of the non-Jewish Early Church Fathers after the death of the Jewish Apostles). This teaching held that God had done away with the Law since Yeshua was the **"fulfillment"** of the Law. The dispensationalist teaching resulted in a new definition of grace – a definition in which a person could accept Yeshua as Savior and yet continue in gross sin. This dispensationalist teaching spread and continues to be spread because Darby's theory is included in the *Schofield Reference Bible*, an extremely popular version of the Bible.

An unfortunate result is the Church teaches that as believers we don't have to keep the Law, as defined in the Older Testament; rather, we are to follow only that which is reiterated in the New Testament - the **"law of Christ"** (Galatians 6:2 -

25

NASB). This is interpreted by many theologians to mean that what was repeated in the New Testament from the Old is to be followed - and if it is not repeated in the New, it was dispensed with by the **"law of Christ."**

For instance, they argue the fact that since the specific day of the Sabbath is not as clearly pointed out in the New Testament as it is in the Old, this leaves it open under the **"law of Christ"** to become any day of the week. They argue that as long as we keep the "principles of the Sabbath," that is, we rest every seventh day, then any day can become our Sabbath. The dangers of following man's principles rather than God's commandments is that "principles" can allow us to listen to God's Law and then do whatever we want.

This is the very reason Yeshua criticized the Pharisees: they held to traditions of men thus invalidating the commandments of God (Mark 7:6-13).

Yeshua answered them, "Yesha'yahu was right when he prophesied about you hypocrites - as it is written, 'These people honor me with their lips, but their hearts are far from me. Their worship of me is useless, because they teach man-made rules as if they were doctrines.'

"You depart from God's command and hold onto human tradition. Indeed, " he said unto them, "you have made a fine art of departing from God's command in order to keep your tradition!" For Moshe said, 'Honor your father and your mother,' and 'Anyone who curses his father or mother must be put to death.' But you say, 'If someone says to his father or mother, "I have promised as a korban"" (that is, as a gift to God) ""what I might have used to help you.' then you no longer let him do anything for his father or mother. Thus, with your tradition which you had handed down to you, you nullify the Word of God! And you do other things like this."

Let me clarify by giving you an example:

Let's say that a father tells his teenage son that he can go out on a date, but he "must be home by midnight." So the son agrees and goes out, yet does not come home until two in the morning.

If we then follow the logic of keeping principles and not commandments, the son could have said: "Well, I did what you said, Dad, I 'came home' as you instructed me!" True, he did "come home;" however, he disobeyed the commandment because he wasn't "home by midnight!"

Let me place this example side-by-side with God's commandment for the seventh-day Sabbath to see how man's principles can cause people to violate God's literal commandments.

Here's the commandment in Exodus 20:10:

but the seventh day is a Shabbat for Adonai your God. On it, you are not to do any kind of work - not you, your son or your daughter, not your male or female slave, not your livestock, and not the foreigner staying with you inside the gates to your property.

The commandment specified "the" seventh day not "a" seventh day or "any" seventh day. It is clear from Genesis 2:2-3 about which day of the week God is speaking. He is talking about "the" seventh day from which He rested from His work of creation, the day He sanctified (set apart). He didn't sanctify just any day of the week, and therefore, we can't call just any day of the week the "Lord's Day!" In fact, Isaiah 58:13 tells us that the Sabbath (the seventh day) is God's holy day - not Sunday!

Now let's backtrack a moment and place the commandment of the father to the son and the commandment of the Lord to us side-by-side. In the father's commandment, he said, "You must be home by midnight." In God's commandment, He said, "Rest on the seventh day."

The son came home and said, "Well, I came home!" The Body of Messiah today says, "Well, I am keeping the Sabbath (Sunday)!" To the son's statement the father responds, "But, you didn't come home *when* I said!" Just so Yeshua looks at the Church's observance and says:

You depart from God's command and hold onto human tradition. Indeed, "he said to them, "you have made a fine art of departing from God's command in order to keep your tradition!" (Mark 7:8-9)

Let's also look at an example in the Older Testament to see what happened to a man who kept the principle of God's command, while skirting the commandment. In 1 Samuel 15:1-26, the Lord commands Saul to totally destroy the Amalekites and put their property under ban. Saul goes out and destroys all the Amalekites saving one: Agag. He also chose to spare the best of the sheep, cattle, the fat beasts, the lambs and everything he deemed worth keeping. However, what was determined to be useless and valueless was destroyed – verses 8-10.

When confronted by Samuel, Saul tried to justify himself by saying, **"I did too pay attention to what Adonai said, and I carried out the mission on which Adonai sent me. I brought back Agag the king of 'Amalek, and I completely destroyed 'Amalek. But the people took some of the spoil, the best of the sheep and cattle set aside for destruction, to sacrifice to Adonai your God in Gilgal."** (Verse 20-21)

Can we say that the Body of Messiah is justified in keeping their traditional sabbath, which the Lord did not command, any more than was Saul, for adding to the Lord's command? Should the father in our story say to the son, "Well done, my good and faithful son; you kept the principles of my commandment. Come into your home and the rest I prepared for you."

How many fathers would accept that principle? Even those who strongly advocate the keeping of "principles" would see that wouldn't fly! Yet, the Church advocates the keeping of the "principle of the Sabbath," that is any day of the week!

Likewise, other directives from the Old Testament that are not mentioned in the New are dealt with in the same manner. For example, God says **"make for yourself twisted cords on the four corners of the garment you wrap around yourself."** (Deuteronomy 22:12), **"not to wear clothing woven with two kinds of thread, wool and linen together"** (Deuteronomy 22:11), **"write [His Words] on the doorframes of your house and on your gates"** (Deuteronomy 11:20), to name a few, yet, we are told these things no longer apply under the **"law of Christ"** because they are not found in the New Testament.

However, if we are to argue a point from the silence of the New Testament on a particular matter, we open ourselves to gross immorality which the Old Testament did not condone.

Let me give you an example: It is true that the Older Testament is much more specific than the Newer relative to various kinds of immoral sexual behavior. Are we to infer from the New Testament's silence on a specific form of immoral sexual behavior that such practice, once specifically forbidden in the Old Testament, is now permissible under the **"Law of Christ?"**

The New Testament laws do not specifically forbid mating with animals, as does the Old, yet, what Christian would say that such silence in the New Testament constitutes implicit consent to the allowance of such practice? Heaven forbid!

The question must be asked: "Must the New Testament be as specific as the Older about every commandment of God in order to make the commandment accepted practice in Christian circles?" Answer: "Why should it?" If God commanded it numerous times - should it not be a *given* that the commandment is to be obeyed whether or not it is specified in the Newer Testament?

Now, let's examine the commandment of the seventh-day Sabbath. Nowhere in the New Testament does the exact day of the Sabbath get specified as it does in the Old Testament (and may I add, nowhere is it clearly and specifically changed to the first day of the week in the Newer, either), and there is absolutely no doubt as to which day is the Sabbath within the many passages in the Torah.By the time of the writing of the New Testament, the Jewish people had a couple thousand years of the seventh-day Sabbath to practice. Therefore, the practice was intact up to the time of Yeshua.(As you'll note, nowhere in the writings of the Gospels did Yeshua ever argue with the religious leaders of His day as to which day was the Sabbath; it was a given!) Yet, we are told to believe that if the New Testament doesn't mention a specific commandment practiced in the Old, we don't have to follow it!

However, the reverse side of the coin, the New Testament doesn't specifically mention tithing yet many pastors use the Old Testament book of Malachi (3:6-12) to encourage tithing in their churches!

Again, it all boils down to a "pick and choose" mentality which permeates the Believing community.If it suits their purpose, then the Scripture apples; if it doesn't suit their purpose, it has been "done away" with in the Old Testament. No wonder the world calls us a bunch of hypocrites!

Before going on I can already see people picking up stones and saying, "Legalist, we're not under the Law but under grace." I respond by saying, "True, but grace is not license to sin (Romans 6:1-2), and since sin is violation of Torah (1 John 3:4), we as believers shouldn't be nullifying or transgressing the law of God, rather **confirming it** (Romans 3:31). This means, we keep it out of our love of God, and not ignore it."

Let us reason together: since the God who created the universe (Genesis 1) and gave the law on Sinai (Exodus 19 and 20) is love (1 John 4:16), we who are indwelt with His Spirit (1 Corinthians 6:19) should be walking in obedience to the Law as He (Yeshua) did (1 John 2:1-6). This is because the Law is holy, righteous and good (Romans 7:12), and reflects the nature of God who is love (Romans 13:8-10). Love, reflected in obedience to God's commandments, should be a natural outgrowth of the new relationship we gain as believers. Scripture says:

"If you love Me, you will keep My commands" (John 14:15).

How does a person know that he or she has this new relationship and has come to know God? 1 John 2:3-7 says:

The way we can be sure we know him is if we are obeying his commands. Anyone who says, "I know him," but doesn't obey his commands is a liar the truth is not in him. But if someone does what he says, then truly love for God has been brought to its goal in him. This is how we are sure that we are united with him. A person who claims to be continuing in union with him ought to conduct his life the way he did.

Furthermore, obedience to His commandments is not the bondage nor the burden that some teach (1 John 5:2,3):

Here is how we know that we love God's children: when we love God, we also do what he commands. For loving God means obeying his commands. Moreover his commands are not burdensome,

It is important to remember that we don't obtain our righteousness from the keeping of the Law (that's an aspect of legalism); the Bible has never taught that - unless, of course, you can keep all the Law all the time (Deuteronomy 6;25).

This we can never do, since we **"all have sinned and come short of earning God's praise"** (Romans 3:23). **For a person who keeps the whole Torah, yet stumbles at one point, has become guilty of breaking them all** (James 2:10). That's why God's grace (Hebrew "chesed") is so important in the life of a believer. Grace doesn't say, "Oh, go on violating God's commandments; it's all paid for by the blood of Yeshua." No, grace says, "Since it is a certainty that we will all violate the law, because we have faith in God and His atonement for us, we will be saved not condemned.

31

In other words, the law does not save a person or make such a person righteous, unless he or she is able to keep the Law always! So, because of the weakness of our flesh, we find it impossible to keep all, much less always, hence we are lost and in need of salvation.

Yeshua provides salvation through the offering of Himself, since He kept all the Law always. He showed His own righteousness with respect to the law and His ability to act as a substitute for us who do not keep the Law always. Through His sacrifice of life, He condemned sin in the flesh setting us free from the law of sin and death.

Therefore, there is no longer any condemnation awaiting those who are in union with the Messiah Yeshua. Why? Because the Torah of the Spirit, which produces this life in union with Messiah Yeshua, has set me free from the "Torah" of sin and death. For what the Torah could not do by itself, because it lacked the power to make the old nature cooperate, God did by sending his own Son as a human being with a nature like our own sinful one. God did this in order to deal with sin, and in so doing he executed the punishment against sin in human nature so that the just requirement of the Torah might be fulfilled in us who do not run our lives according to what our old nature wants but according to what the Spirit wants. (Romans 8:1-4)

Allow me to clarify a serious misconception of the Church at this juncture: the Torah (or Law) given by God on Sinai is *not* the law of sin and death - contrary to contemporary Christian theology.

In the preceding chapter of Romans, Shaul says the **"Torah is holy; that is, the commandment is holy, just and good."** (Romans 7, verses 12, 13).

No, it is not the Law (Torah) which is the law of sin and death, rather, it is another law which exists in the members of my body that is of sin and death.

But in my various parts, I see a different "Torah," one that battles with the Torah in my mind and makes me a prisoner of sin's "Torah," which is operating in my various parts. What a miserable creature I am! Who will rescue me from this body bound for death? Thanks be to God, he will! - through Yeshua the Messiah, our Lord! (Romans 7: 23-25).

Notice in these verses that we are talking about two distinct laws – one is the law of the flesh, and the other the Law of God.

And, though we know that we can't keep the Law of God thereby obtaining our righteousness, does that mean that we shouldn't try at all? Heavens no! Notice in the preceding verses how Sha'ul desired to keep God's Law? It should be even so with every believer the earnest desire to keep God's Law and not the law of sin found within the members of our bodies. Wherever sin (the transgressions of God's Laws) is found, it needs to be uprooted and destroyed.

I believe that there are three basic reasons why we break God's commandments (sin):

1) Through Ignorance/Not Knowing. Most often, we break God's commandments through ignorance; that is, we honestly don't know what His commandments are or how they apply to us. I don't know many true believers in Yeshua who consciously want to rebel against God by saying: "Well, I know this behavior is prohibited but I'm going to spite God and do it anyway, 'cause I'm saved by grace and not by works.'"

In all fairness, most believers *do* have a love for God and want to please Him. To avoid this type of transgression, we must study the Word of God as the Apostle Sha'ul says to Timothy in 2 Timothy 3:16-17:

All Scripture is God-breathed and is valuable for teaching the truth, convicting of sin, correcting faults and training

in right living; thus anyone who belongs to God may be fully equipped for every good work.

It is important to remember that at the time of this writing, the New Testament was not yet complete.What Sha'ul was referring to was the writings found in the Older Testament. Somehow, in the minds of most believers, they relate this passage to the New Testament only. The approximate dates of the Newer Covenant writings is as follows:

Book	Approximate Date	Author
Mark	50-70 Common Era (C.E.)	John Mark, a disciple of Peter
Mattityahu (Matthew)	55-75 C.E.	Matthew/Levi, the Apostle
Luke	59-75 C.E.	Luke
Yochanon (John)	53-110 C.E.	Yochanon (John), 'whom Yeshua loved'
Acts	63-70 C.E.	Luke
1 Thessalonians	51 C.E.	Shaul (Paul)
2 Thessalonians	52 C.E.	Shaul
Galatians	53 C.E.	Shaul
1 & 2 Corinthians	55 C.E.	Shaul
Romans	57 C.E.	Shaul
Colossians	60 C.E.	Shaul
Ephesians	60 C.E.	Shaul
Philemon	60 C.E.	Shaul
Phillipians	61 C.E.	Shaul
James (Yaakov)	63 C.E.	Yaakov, the brother of Yeshua
1 Timothy	63 C.E.	Shaul
Titus	63 C.E.	Shaul

1 & 2 Peter (Kefa)	65-68 C.E.	Shimon Kefa (Simon Peter)
2 Timothy	66 C.E.	Shaul
Hebrews	65-70 C.E.	Barnabas, Apollos?
1,2,3 Yochanon (John)	85-96 C.E.	Yochanon, (John) the Apostle
Jude	65-80 C.E.	Judah/Judas the brother of Yeshua
Revelation	95 C.E.	Yochanon, (John) the Apostle

In brief, if the Older Covenant was a good enough standard for Sha'ul to recommend to Timothy, then is it not good enough for us today? It still speaks to us of what is sin and how to receive forgiveness for our sins.

We repent of our sin when we read God's Word and He convicts us of our sins by the power of the Holy Spirit (John 16:8). It is the Holy Spirit's job to convict us of sin; it is our job to study His Word and find our God's position on a particular matter.

2) Through Misinformation/Being Mistold. We can find several examples in Scripture where people have added to the Word of God with disastrous results. The first one that comes to mind is the original sin in the Garden of Eden. In Genesis 3:3, we see three seemingly innocuous words **"nor touch it"** added to the original prohibition of Genesis 2:17. While it is not certain who added these words, whether Adam in trying to prevent Eve from touching the tree, or Eve through a misunderstanding by Adam (since Adam received the commandment before Eve was fashioned).Nonetheless, the principle is absolute: whenever we add to, or subtract from, God's commandments and "principlize" it, we run contrary to the Word of Almighty God. That's why we are expressly commanded not to alter it by adding to, or subtracting from, God's Word:

In order to obey the mitzvot of Adonai your God which I am giving to you, do not add to what I am saying, and do not subtract from it. (Deuteronomy 4:2).

I warn everyone hearing the words of the prophecy in this book that if anyone adds to them, God will add to him the plagues written in this book. And if anyone takes anything away from the words in the bok of this prophecy, God will take away his share in the Tree of Life and the holy city, as described in this book. (Revelation 22:18, 19).

It is a serious thing to add to, or subtract from, God's Word. The consequences resulting from Adam and Eve's adding to God's Word resulting in sin have affected all mankind, even to this day.It did not matter that the error came about as a misunderstanding or mistelling, the price of sin was death. Likewise, the result of adding to or subtracting to God's commandments by believers today will reap the same consequences.

On Judgement Day, we can't simply point a finger at our theologian or pastor and say, "Well, he told me it wasn't a sin." They are not God. They will not be standing at your side to defend you. You can't say, "It's their fault." No, we will each be held responsible for finding the truth of the Scriptures.

No man has the authority to change God's Word. Even Yeshua did not change God's Word or Law, though He had the authority as God Incarnate to do so! Matthew 5:17-19 affirms Yeshua' position on the Law. He said that He did not come to abolish or destroy the Law, but to fulfill it:

Don't think that I have come to abolish the Torah or the Prophets. I have come not to abolish but to complete. Yes indeed! I tell you that until heaven and earth pass away, not so much as a yud or a stroke will pass from the Torah - not until everything that must happen has happened. So whoever disobeys the least of these mitzvot and teaches others to do so will be called least in the Kingdom of Heaven.

David Bivin and Roy Blizzard, Jr. in their book, *Understanding the difficult words of Jesus,* seek to address a misunderstanding in the body of Messiah regarding the terms "abolish" and "fulfill":

In Matthew 5:17, Jesus claims he has no intention of abolishing or suspending the Mosaic Law. For most Christians, this comes as a shock. After all, did not the Apostle Paul say, "Christ is the end of the Law" (Romans 10:4)? Jesus' statement seems such a contradiction that many Christian commentators have tried to explain it away by suggesting that his words do not really mean what they seem to mean. Their attempts are futile.

The meaning of Jesus' words is clear. As long as the world lasts, he goes on to say in verse 18, the Law will last. Here Jesus is in complete agreement with the Rabbis: "Everything has an end heaven and earth have an end except one thing which has no end. And what is that? The Law" (Genesis Rabbah 10: 1); "No letter will ever be abolished from the Law" (Exodus Rabbah 6:1); "Should the world unite to uproot one word of the Law, they would be unable to do it" (Leviticus Rabbah 19:2).

... Undoubtedly, in trying to understand this passage, everything hinges on the meaning of the words "destroy" and "fulfill" in verse 17. What does Jesus mean by "destroying the Law" and "fulfilling the Law".

"Destroy" and "fulfill" are technical terms used in rabbinical argumentation. When a rabbi felt that a colleague had misinterpreted a passage of Scripture, he would say, "You are destroying the Law!" Needless to say, in most cases his colleague strongly disagreed. What was "destroying the Law" for one rabbi, was "fulfilling the Law" (correctly interpreting Scripture) for another.

What we see in Matthew 5:17ff. is a rabbinical discussion. Someone has accused Jesus of "destroying" the Law. Of course, neither Jesus nor his accuser would ever think of literally destroying the Law. Furthermore, it would never enter the accuser's mind to charge Jesus with intent to abolish part or all of the Mosaic Law. What is being called into question is Jesus' system of interpretation, the way he interprets Scripture.

When accused, Jesus strongly denies that his method of interpreting "destroys" or weakens its meaning. He claims, on the contrary, to be more orthodox than his accuser. For Jesus, a "light" commandment ("Do not bear hatred in your heart") is as important as a "heavy" commandment ("Do not murder"). And a disciple who breaks even a "light" commandment will be considered "light" (have an inferior position) in Jesus' movement (Matthew 5:19).

"Never imagine for a moment," Jesus says, "that I intend to abrogate the Law by misinterpreting it. My intent is not to weaken or negate the Law, but by proper interpreting God's written Word I aim to establish it, that is, make it even more lasting. I would never invalidate the Law by effectively removing something from it through misinterpretation.

Heaven and earth would sooner disappear than something disappear from the Law. Not the smallest letter in the alphabet, the yod, nor even its decorative spur, will ever disappear from the Law.[6]

Furthermore He warns us against anyone who nullifies even the least of the commandments and so teaches others. **"If anyone disobeys the least of these mitzvot,"** He says, **"he will be**

6 *Understanding the difficult words of Jesus*, David Bivin & Roy Blizzard, Jr., CENTER FOR BIBLICAL ANALYSIS, Division of DESTINY IMAGE PUBLISHERS, Shippensburg, PA, Copyright 1984, pages 154-155

called least in the Kingdom of Heaven. But whoever obeys them and so teaches others will be called great in the Kingdom of Heaven.

If there is any New Testament passage that wholeheartedly supports what was written in the Law in the lives of believers, this is it. This means that no one short of God Himself has the authority to annul, abolish, destroy, change, or set aside the Law — not Peter, not Sha'ul, not Ya'akov, nor any other man. And since Yeshua didn't do it, then no one else has the authority to do it either!

Those who say that Sha'ul's writings support an anti-Nomian (anti-Law) stance have only to look back to Yeshua' statement in Matthew 5. If Sha'ul was against the keeping of the Law in the life of a New Testament believer, then he *is* least in the kingdom of heaven! (I personally do not believe that he is anti-Law, nor least in the kingdom.)

3) Through Willful Disobedience/To Know what is right yet deliberately transgress. (James 4:17).

This is the most dangerous position for a believer (or anyone else) to take. Such behavior is rebelliousness, and 1 Samuel 15:23 equates rebelliousness with the sin of witchcraft. Unfortunately, there are some in the Body of Messiah who are rebellious. Heaven help the rebellious saint!

The reason why Yeshua couldn't perform miracles in His hometown of Nazareth was because of unbelief (Mark 6:5,6), for which the underlying cause was *rebellion* to what God wanted to do there.

Likewise, if we wonder why the believing community of today has lost the power of the First Century Believing community, we need only look at our deliberate fall from God's standards of holiness. I believe the greatest reason why the Body of Messiah today does not exhibit the power and miracles as seen in the First Century is because it is not a holy people by God's definition. The farther away we get from the original, the weaker we become. Allow me to illustrate. When Moses left the mountain after communing with God, his face glowed so much that he had to wear a cloth to veil it. As time passed, the glow began to diminish. So it is with us as we depart the holiness of God. Exposure to God's holiness produces power. The farther away we are, the less power we exhibit.

If we liken the body of Messiah to a conduit of God's power, and our corruption as corrosion within the conduit, we can easily see how the more corrupted and corroded the believing community becomes, the less God's power and love can flow through her. What we in the body of Messiah need is a good, healthy dose of spiritual "Liquid Plumber." We need to get the centuries of accumulated rebelliousness burnt out of us so that God can once again use us as He used the believer in the First Century! It means that we have to get back to Biblical standards, following God's Law under the empowerment of His Holy Spirit!

Then, I believe we'll see miracles as never seen in nearly 1,800 years; the dead shall rise, the lame shall walk, the deaf shall hear, the captives shall be set free; not as an exception, but as the norm! And it will be coming through everyday, holy believers, and not fake preachers and televangelists.

Yeshua said that we as a body of Messiah should be doing *greater* things than He did as He walked the earth (John 14:12)! The signs and wonders following the believers should be the *norm*, not the *exception!* Today's believing community finds just the opposite to be true! Have we lost something as the Body of Messiah? You should believe we have! We have lost the standard of holiness to which we have been called. We are not to be holy in title or name only, but to partake of the Divine Nature, which is holy.

How are we to know what "holy" is? Since He is much greater than we, look to His Word. Yeshua, that Word, walked in the holiness that was His nature as God, and that is how we are to walk. We are to walk in the same manner (1 John 2) and the *evidence* of our being a true believer is that we are holy, keeping His commandments- not seeking justification, but, rather, out of a sincere heartfelt love for God.

Sha'ul in Romans 7:12 speaks of the Law as being holy; that is, the commandment is holy, just and good. The Law, being a reflection of the nature of God, is the written standard of what "holy" is, and we are commanded to as God is holy (Leviticus 11: 44,45), an unending *unchanging* holiness.

This means that we have to go back to what God defines as holy in the Law and not what we think is holy; we can call anything "holy," but that doesn't make it so. As stated before, holiness is a state of being, not a title. The bottom line is this: either God's Word in its entirety is pertinent to the people of God today, or else it isn't; let's not pussyfoot in the willows of theology. God wants His people to be holy, and He isn't going to change His standards in order to accommodate our theology.His standards are based upon His unchanging character (Malachi 3:6), and *we* must conform if we are to be like Him.

Dr. Daniel C. Juster in his book, *Growing to Maturity A Messianic Jewish Guide* offers thoughtful insight on the biblical marks of holiness a believer should have:

1. A holy person is one who has died to self. **Yeshua said,**

"If anyone would come after Me, he must deny himself and take up his cross daily and follow Me. For whoever wants to save his life will lose it, but whoever loses his life for me will save it. What good is it for a man to gain the whole world, and yet lose or forfeit his very self?" (Luke 9:23-25)

In Scripture, to lose self does not mean to lose personal identity. It means to lose self-seeking motivations. When we identify with the death and resurrection of Yeshua, we

41

replace selfish motives with motives of unselfish love and compassion. We love God with all our hearts and our neighbors as ourselves...

2. A holy person is a person of compassionate love (agape). This second characteristic is simply implied from the first characteristic.

3. A holy person reflects God's standards of righteousness in the Bible. Because Messiah is in us, Paul said the way of faith fulfills the law (Romans 3:31). The believer does not sin so grace may abound, but he understands grace as the power of righteousness (e.g., he reflects honesty in business, love for the poor, and honoring the aged)...

4. A holy person does not lust for material possessions. Scripture promises that God will abundantly provide whatever we need for whatever He calls us to do. If His calling includes material gifts of wealth, we praise Him and use our wealth for His Kingdom. If not, we still praise Him...

5. A holy person is called to holy and pure thinking. God's standard of holiness includes purity of thought. Scripture teaches that out of the heart (the thought center), flow "evil thoughts, murder, adultery, sexual immorality, theft, false testimony, slander. These are what make a man "'unclean'" (Matthew 15:19,20)...

6. The holy person is called to purity of speech. The biblical standard for speech is summarized in Ephesians 4: 29,30. Speech flows from thought.

"Do not let any unwholesome talk come out of our mouths, but only what is helpful for building others up (edify) according to their needs, that it may benefit those who listen. And do not grieve the Holy Spirit of God, with whom you were sealed for the day of redemption."

7. The holy person is called to humility. Genuine holiness cannot be maintained apart from humility. The proud person may externally follow some of the rules of holiness but will project a self-righteousness, holier-than-thou attitude. Humility is not self-depreciation. Selfdepreciation is a manifestation of insecurity and self-rejection. Humility is an attitude of dependence and gratitude toward God...

8. The holy person is a socially compassionate person. Nothing is clearer from a study of the prophets than the fact that God seeks legal and economic justice for the poor, widowed, orphaned, and alienated. We do not endorse a particular philosophy. Honest believers differ as to which plans will work. But what they must not differ in is that Christians are called to be advocates of social justice and compassion. A holy person is also honest and compassionate in his own financial dealings.[7]

When we look at these characteristics, we see that they are beyond the capabilities of human effort.Of course, we may see some of these characteristics in people of the world, such as social compassion, purity of speech, and rejection of material or sexual lusts; but no one can fulfill all these without the power of God indwelling them.

True holiness, therefore, cannot be attained by the efforts of men. Instead, it is attained when men surrender themselves to the Holy One, Who then indwells them with His Holy Spirit and causes them to live holy lives.

When the Body of Messiah repents and turns back to Him and His standards as found in His Word, we will return to an understanding of what it means to be holy.

7   *Growing to Maturity A Messianic Jewish Guide*, Dr. Daniel C. Juster, The Union of Messianic Jewish Congregations Press, Gaithersburg, MD, Copyright 1982, 1985, 1987, pages 72- 77 31

Chapter 3

The Overall Picture

In looking at this critical subject correctly, it is necessary to look at what the entire Bible says about the Law, not just what the New Testament says about it. Let me ask you a simple question: Could you pick up a novel, read only the last half of it and understand the entire story? Hardly. You'll come out with an incomplete picture of the whole story and you may even miss the real purpose intended by the author.

In similar vein, to formulate a theology about the Laws of God based upon the New Testament writings alone is like being led blindfolded into a studio, placed inches in front of a large picture and upon removal of the blindfold, being expected to describe the entire picture.

Follow along and see what I mean. The picture following is just a small portion of a much larger one. Can you give a complete and perfect description of the subject? It's kind of hard to, isn't it? Yet, it is world renowned. If we take this part of the picture away from the context of the whole, we risk coming to the wrong conclusion of our subject. This, dear friend, is exactly the case when we form a theology about such an important subject as the Law of God by taking only the writings of the New Testament (without the foundation laid by the Old Testament) on the subject and concluding that the Law is not valid in the lives of believers today. This is particularly true of Sha'ul's writings which many take to be anti-nomian (anti-Law) in nature.

This is why the theologies of many churches today are anti-Law. The passages of the New Testament are made to stand separate from the context of the whole of Scripture; hence, the resulting errant, dangerous conclusion: the Law is no longer valid as a standard of holiness and no longer rules for believers in Yeshua since, as the Church teaches, "He fulfilled the Law and placed us under grace."

However, this is not what the whole of the Bible teaches regarding the Law, nor what the Apostles actually lived and taught as recorded in the Scriptures. What we need to do is to place the New Testament writings back into the context of the whole of Biblical writings and then interpret the New Testament in the light of the Older Testament. We then come to a full, complete and perfect conclusion.

In similar manner, when we place that one section of our picture back into the whole, we have a full and complete picture; and we can give an adequate description of the Dome of the

Rock on the Temple Mount in Jerusalem. Likewise, when we place the New Testament writings within the context of the whole Scripture, we see the continuous call of God back to Himself and back to obedience to His commandments.

If a single prophet of God said, "Oh, we can have a perfectly acceptable relationship with God even if we don't keep His commandments," he would have been regarded as a false prophet by the people, since the Scripture abundantly makes it clear otherwise. Why should the New Testament writers be treated differently? If a New Testament writer said that, should he be treated as a true prophet of God? No! But in fact, we will not find a single apostle, Sha'ul included, saying that we can have a perfectly acceptable relationship with God and be disobedient to His commandments. Particularly since God ties obedience to His commandments with holiness.

To lay a foundation for what the whole of Scripture says on the subject of holiness, we will devote the next section to specific Biblical references regarding God's Law and commandments, for only in so doing will we find God's blueprint for how we are to live a holy life.

Chapter 4

The Scriptures and the Law

It is not surprising that whenever the Law and commandments are mentioned in Scripture, the majority of those Scriptures speak of the pertinence and observance of those Laws by God's people.Some of the passages found in the Old Testament speak of certain Mosaic commandments and observances as **"perpetual," "forever,"** or **"throughout your generations."**

This means that, despite claims by some Christians that all the Mosaic Law has been fulfilled by Messiah and is, therefore, "done away with," there are certain commandments that will never be done away with. Certain Levitical observances, including the commandment to observe the seventh day as the Sabbath (Exodus 31:16,17) fell into this category. "Forever" doesn't end through fulfillment.

It may be necessary for some of us to realize that since the Scriptures are Jewish, in order to understand them we need to go back to the Jewish "roots" of our faith fully. This means that we must understand how the Jewish people viewed Scripture; rather than how the Greeks interpreted Scripture.

For instance, why is it that the Jewish people still observe the seventh day Sabbath rest? They do so because God commanded it **"forever."** Does anyone have the authority to change God's commandment? Yes, God who gave it, or Yeshua – God Incarnate, but neither does so. If neither God nor Yeshua revised or altered the seventh day rest, none of the Disciples had the authority to do so, either. Notice I didn't say worship, we can worship ANY day in Judaism. But, on the Sabbath day we are commanded by God to **rest**. However, keep in mind that in an agricultural society, it naturally follows that the day on which one rests is most probably the only time one is able to find time to worship.

It doesn't matter how sentimental we think the Apostles were in honoring His birth or His resurrection, what matters is, did they authorize or have the authority to authorize changes in the commandments that God had specified in His Word? Not if what Yeshua said about the Law in Matthew 5 is still true! Rather, their teachings supported what preceding Scripture had already stated.

When Sha'ul went to Berea, he went into the synagogue of the Jews (Acts 17:10-12):

But as soon as night fell, the brothers sent Sha'ul and Sila off to Berea. As soon as they arrived, they went to the synagogue. Now the people here were of nobler character than the ones in Thessalonica; they eagerly welcomed the message, checking the Tanakh every day to see if the things Sha'ul was saying were true.

As Sha'ul taught them about the good news of the Gospel of Yeshua, they checked the Older Testament passages (remember, New Testament Scripture was not written at that time) to see whether these teachings were true (verse 11). If Sha'ul had countermanded or nullified anything that was commanded in Scripture, he would have been furiously rejected by the Bereans. Why? Because God forbade Israel from listening to a "prophet" who led them away from the God they already knew (Deuteronomy 13). The God they knew exhorted them through all His prophets to keep His commandments! It must be strongly emphasized that though Sha'ul was accused of violating the Law of Moses by commanding Jews to forsake Moses, not to circumcise their children and not to walk according to the customs, he puts this to rest before all the other Apostles in Acts 21:16-26, when he shows his obedience to Torah and keeps the Nazirite vow (Numbers 6). Here, Sha'ul, the man **"not under the Law"** (1 Corinthians 9:20- New American Standard Bible), having been accused of violating the Law, shows how he "stays in line and keep the Torah" (Acts 21:24), so that everyone will know that there is nothing to these rumors which they have heard about you (Sha'ul)."

Was Sha'ul lying to the other Disciples when he observed this Mosaic Law or was he a hypocrite? I believe he was neither! Sha'ul, who confronted Kefa about hypocrisy (Galatians 2:11-21), would never have resorted to hypocrisy before council in Jerusalem, nor would he lie; that would have been a blatant sin for which he would have been challenged by the other disciples. Instead, there is a third possibility: Sha'ul, in his writings, is being misunderstood - either through ignorance, or possibly through malevolent deliberation. Kefa leaves this possibility open in 2 Peter 3:15-17 when he says and think of our Lord's patience as deliverance, just as our dear brother Sha'ul also wrote you, following the wisdom God gave him. Indeed, he speaks about these things in all his letters. They contain some things that are hard to understand, things which the uninstructed and unstable distort, to their own destruction, as they do the other Scriptures.

Kefa here affirms Sha'ul's letters as on par with the rest of Scripture which, as you see in his personal obedience to the Law, affirm the continuity and observance of the Law. Yet, he confirms that Sha'ul's writings are hard to understand.

Since it stands to reason that Sha'ul's writings are virtually the only passages seemingly at issue with regard to the Law, could it be that the Believing community today is following in the traditions of the **"uninstructed,"**and **"unstable"** men who Kefa was writing about?

I believe so... How could a believing community that was entirely Jewish and observant of the Law of Moses change to a non-Jewish, non-observant one? I believe the answer is a simple one. As time passed and as the Jewish leadership died through martyrdom or natural causes, the leadership of the Body of

Messiah passed to the group of men who were in numerical superiority – the Platonic, non- Jews who did not understand Jewish thought and, furthermore, were in many cases anti-Semitic.

Following the New Testament era, one of the first heresies that the Church faced was propounded by Marcion. He was a wealthy shipowner from Sinope (in what is now northern Turkey) who came to Rome. About A.D. 138, Marcion began to argue that the Old Testament was inferior to the New and hence had no part of authoritative revelation. He therefore fought to have it removed from the canon.

To some degree, Marcion appears to have been influenced by the dualistic teachings of Gnosticism. Thus he held that the world, with its appalling evils, was created by a Demiurge (a term Gnostics borrowed from Platonism). This cruel god of battles and bloody sacrifices, so Marcion contended, was revealed in the pages of the Old Testament. He insisted that since an evil world could not be created by a good God, the Old Testament was really the Demiurge's book and hence of lesser status than the New. The Old was the great antithesis of the New and thus was demeaned as being imperfect, offensive, and unedifying.

But the New Testament, Marcion insisted, revealed the true God in the coming of Christ from heaven. Unlike the Demiurge, this God was a God of love. Marcion argued that the New Testament, being Christ's book (not that of the Demiurge), was unquestionably superior to the Old Testament. Furthermore, in his quest to demote the Old Testament from its recognized position of authority, he began to extol the writings of Paul, which held that Christians were "free from the Law" (cf. Gal. 5:1). He contended firmly that the church was wrong in attempting to combine the gospel with Judaism. Indeed, Marcion's principal goal was to rid

Christianity of every trace of Judaism. Hence, Marcion became known as the archenemy or the "Jew God."[8]

Though the Church rejected Marcion's views as heresy, it nonetheless had adopted much of his attitudes toward the Older Testament. As Dr. Wilson observes:

Though often cunningly concealed, in today's Church rather strong vestiges of Marcionism have survived. But we are polite. Hardly aware of its subtle presence, we do not call it "Neo- Marcionism," "heresy," or "anti-Judaism." Nevertheless, in our concerted effort to be "New Testament" believers, we have all too often unconsciously minimized the place and importance of the Old Testament and Church's Hebraic roots. At worst, many so called Bible-believing Christians have become de facto "quarter-of-the-Bible" adherents (the New Testament has 260 chapters compared to the Old Testament's 929 chapters); at best, they rely on a "loose-leaf" edition of the Old Testament (i.e., they select only a few portions of the Old Testament), in addition to the New Testament. This selectivity has had the effect of neglecting the totality of written revelation, severing the Hebrew roots of the Christian faith, and thus eroding the full authority of the Holy Scriptures.

In addition to relegating the old Testament to secondary importance in preaching and teaching, Neo-Marcionism continues to plague today's Church in other ways. For instance, it is often found in those theological circles where the displacement or supersession theory is taught concerning Israel. This teaching is tantamount to saying that Israel has been permanently cast aside and thus has had no theological relevance for the last nineteen hundred years. In our opinion, this position fails to give satisfactory explanation

---

8 *Our Father Abraham, Jewish Roots of the Christian Faith*, Dr. Marvin R. Wilson, copyright 1989, Wm. B. Eerdman's Publishing Co., Grand Rapids, MI, pages 108- 109

to Paul's argument that "a hardening has come upon part of Israel, until the full number of the Gentiles come in, and so all Israel will be saved" (Rom. 11:25-26).

Neo-Marcionism is also manifested in Christian art which tends to downplay, whether consciously or unconsciously, the Jewishness of Jesus and the early Church. This tendency may be as subtle as an artist's depiction of the facial features of Jesus in a non-Jewish way.

Or artwork may overtly display - either ignorantly or deliberately - non-Jewish or anti-Jewish subject matter, for example, the sculpturing of an uncircumcised infant Jesus, or the Last Supper scene with no common cup of wine or the disciples in a seated, rather than reclining, posture.

Neo-Marcionism also tends to be advanced when a church communicates to a nearby synagogue the impression, "We don't have anything to learn from you and your dead, legalistic religion, but you've got everything to learn from us."[9]

These attitudes did not originate out of a vacuum, but came into the Church by those whom the Church calls "the early Church Fathers," namely: Origen, Augustine, Justin Martyr, Eusebius, Constantine, Gregory of Nyssa, John Chrysostom, Jerome and others. These espoused a Platonic (Greek) understanding of the Scripture, and by so doing distorted the original meanings what were written by the hand of Hebrews.

To offer an example of this, in his dialogue with Trypho (a Jew) Justin Martyr said,

For the law promulgated on Horeb is now old, and belongs to you alone; but this is for all universally. Now, law placed against law has abrogated that which is before it, and a covenant which comes after in like manner has put an end to

---

9   *IBID.,* pages 109-110

the previous one; and an eternal and final law - namely, Christ - has been given to us, and the covenant is trustworthy after which there shall be no law, no commandment, no ordinance."[10]

But Justin is wrong, for according to Sha'ul in Galatians 3:15-17:

Brothers, let me make an analogy from everyday life: when someone swears an oath, no one can set it aside or add to it. Now the promises were made to Avraham and to his seed. It doesn't say, "and to seeds," as if to many; on the contrary, it speaks of one - "and to your seed" - and this "one" is the Messiah. Here is what I am saying: the legal part of the Torah, which came into being 430 years later, does not nullify an oath sworn by God, so as to abolish the promise.

The later covenant does NOT abrogate, or nullify, the preceding covenant; instead, if one compares all the covenants of the Bible, the latter expands and enlightens the preceding covenant. This is why Yeshua in Matthew 5 does NOT annul the Law; rather, He expands and enlightens the already-given Law.

Whereas Justin may have erred (as we all do), others such as Eusebius were much more deliberate in their theological distortions. A student of Origen, Eusebius was careful to leave out of his history of the church that which did not fit into his theology:

in writing any book, an author chooses what to include and what to leave out. In writing history, a faithful historian will make these choices so as to present an accurate picture of the past. Eusebius was intentionally inaccurate. He had his own agenda.

No other source might [be] used that contradicted or convicted with the apostolic tradition as Eusebius conceived it.

---

10 *The Ante-Nicene Fathers, Volume 1*, Alexander Roberts & James Donaldson, copyright 1987, WM. B. EERDMANS PUBLISHING CO., page 200

Eusebius ignored the sources that showed the apostolic tradition to be different from what he thought it should be. He was intent on creating an apostolic tradition that was different from what the apostles had actually believed and taught.

...Eusebius was the product of the Alexandrine school of theology [that of Origen]. To him orthodox tradition was primarily just the tradition preserved at Alexandria, in its entirety and without any contradictions.[11]

With regard to our current Christian theology and tradition, how can we be certain that what we today hold to be of apostolic origin and interpretation is *truly* what the Messiah and the apostles taught?

How do we know that it isn't from the traditions of men such as those cited? We're taught to observe Sunday as the Sabbath because "the Apostles observed the first day of the week as the new Sabbath since Yeshua rose from the dead on the first day of the week."

Says who – God inspired Scripture, or traditions of men? Only two passages in the New Testament *specifically* refer to the first day of the week for any gathering, Acts 20:7 and 1 Corinthians 16:2 and, placed within Jewish context, these do not refer to Sunday at all, but, rather to the traditional Jewish Havdalah service observed on Saturday evening when the Sabbath ends. (The Hebrew day goes from sundown to sundown. On Friday evening at sundown, the seventh day [Sabbath] begins. On Saturday evening at sundown, the first day of the week begins) Compare that with the many references to the disciples' observance of the seventh-day Sabbath in the Book of Acts, and it becomes clear from the Scriptures that the lives of the

11 *THE CHURCH AND THE JEWS, The Biblical Relationship*, Daniel Gruber, Copyright 1991, GENERAL COUNCIL OF THE ASSEMBLIES OF GOD, page 9

Apostles were observance to God's commandments. However, from traditional Christian doctrine we get an entirely different view.

In his book, *FROM SABBATH TO SUNDAY,* published in 1987 by the PONTIFICAL GREGORIAN UNIVERSITY PRESS, Samuele Bacchiocchi argues that the change from a Saturday Sabbath to a Sunday Sabbath occurred approximately one century after the death of Messiah and was not a practice of His apostles.

The **"...historical data which we have briefly considered discredit any attempt to make the Jerusalem Church, prior to A.D. 135, the champion of liturgical innovations such as Sunday worship. We have found that of all the Christian Churches, this was seemingly both racially and theologically the one closest and most loyal to Jewish religious traditions."**[12]

Instead, the origin of a Sunday Sabbath was due to the antisemitic dynamic in the Church at Rome, and an interplay of pagan factors resulting in not only a change in the day of rest, but also in a change of its meaning.

"In examining the possible origin of Sunday observance among primitive Jewish-Christians, we have just concluded that it is futile to seek among them for traces of its origin, because of their basic loyalty to Jewish religious customs such as Sabbath-keeping. We shall therefore direct our search for the origin of Sunday to Gentile Christian circles."[13]

He then expounds upon how the Church of Rome proceeded to substitute its holy days in place of the Jewish ones. What is unique about Dr. Bacchiocchi's book is that it is the first book

---

12 *FROM SABBATH TO SUNDAY*, Samuele Bacchiocchi, THE PONTIFICAL GREGORIAN UNIVERSITY PRESS, Rome: Copyright 1977, page 163.

13 *IBID.*, page 165

written by a non-Catholic ever to be published by a Pontifical press with the Catholic imprimatur (approval), the very Church of Rome that caused these changes! In fact, he spent five years at the Pontifical Gregorian University in Rome examining the most reliable documents to come up with his conclusions. His scholarship is impressive and extensive. I would recommend it most highly to those who wish to understand the truth.

As with the Sabbath, all issues need careful Biblical exegesis from a Hebrew perspective. The Body of Messiah must reexamine her Jewish roots and leave man-made traditions to find safer haven in God's commandments. In my personal opinion, it would be better to err on the side of righteousness and keep God's commandments, than to err on the side of those who say, "the Law is fulfilled."

It is extremely important to note that there is NO separate word in First Century Greek to distinguish between "Law" and "legalism." *Both* "Law" and "legalism" use the *same* word in Koine Greek; *"nomos."*

-it will be well to bear in mind the fact (which, so far as we know, had not received attention before it was noted in [Cranfield's article] the Scottish Journal of Theology, Volume 17, 1964, p. 55) that the Greek language of Paul's day possessed no word-group corresponding to our 'legalism,' 'legalist' and 'legalistic.' This means that he lacked a convenient terminology for expressing a vital distinction, and so was surely seriously hampered in the work of clarifying the Christian position with regard to the law. In view of this, we should always, we think, be ready to reckon with the possibility that Pauline statements which at first sight seem to disparage the law, were really directed not against the law itself but against that understanding and misuse of it for which we now have a convenient terminology. In this very difficult terrain, Paul was pioneering. If we make allowances for these circumstances, we shall not be so easily

baffled or misled by a certain impreciseness of statement which we shall sometimes encounter.[14]

That being the case, when Sha'ul speaks negatively of the *"Law,"* could he not just as well be speaking negatively about "legalism" which *is more appropriate?* Legalism is the observance of the Law to seek justification or salvation by it [which can never happen], or as defined by *THE ENCYCLOPEDIA OF THE JEWISH RELIGION:*

The preference of legal rules and norms above moral and spiritual values.[15]

To clarify the difference between"keeping the Law" and "legalism," let me give you an example: Let's assume that a licensed operator of a motor vehicle approaches a stop sign, slows down and stops at the sign. When he thus obeys the law of the land and stops, would he be considered a "legalist?" Of course not! He is simply obeying the law! However, if he stopped at the stop sign, as he is supposed to do, and a police officer sees him stop appropriately, should he expect to be rewarded for his obedience to the law? Does our legal system recognize those who keep the law? Rarely. We'll be waiting a long time if we think we'll be rewarded for keeping the law. However, had he run the stop sign in front of the law officer, he would be rewarded with quite another sort of recognition, and, at the very least, given a ticket for his flagrant disobedience of the law! In the same way, we can understand why Sha'ul would say that the Law was not made for the righteous person (one who keeps the Law), but for the unrighteous (one who breaks the Law).

For we know that the Torah is good, provided one uses it in the way the Torah itself intends.We are aware that Torah is

---

14 *THE INTERNATIONAL CRITICAL COMMENTARY, ROMANS,* Copyright 1979, C.E.B. Cranfield, page 853

15 *THE ENCYCLOPEDIA OF THE JEWISH RELIGION,* page 236

not for a person who is righteous, but for those who are heedless of Torah and rebellious, ungodly and sinful, wicked and worldly, for people who kill their fathers and mothers, for murderers, the sexually immoral - both heterosexual and homosexual - slave dealers, liars, perjurers, and anyone who acts contrary to the sound teaching that accords with the Good News of the glorious and blessed God. (1 Timothy 1:8-10)

Believers who are made righteous through faith should not be lawless and rebellious because the new nature of Yeshua is taking over in their lives enabling them to be obedient to God's Laws. This is the lawful use of the Law.

As we go through these passages, please note the general direction of Scripture: is it for the keeping of God's laws, statutes, and commandments, or is it not? If it speaks of keeping His commandments, what is the motive for the observance and why does God want us to observe it? If it does not speak of observing God's commandments, why not? Maybe it is speaking against the legalistic observance of God's commandments and not against keeping God's commandments through a motive of love for God.

Below are passages that speak directly of the Law, commandments, and statutes. There are perhaps hundreds of other references that could be incorporated in this book to support the keeping of God's commandments, but these are a few which support the original intent of the Law. It would be helpful to go through these passages writing them down as you study them.

OLD TESTAMENT PASSAGES

The Lord gives the Law to His people - The Law was meant to be a gift to us; to benefit us; it was not man-made. If what James 1:17 says is true: **"Every good act of giving and every perfect gift is from above, coming down from the Father who made the heavenly lights; with him there is neither**

variation nor darkness caused by turning," then should not the Law, which also was given from above, be considered "good?" Yeshua speaks in the human sense of giving in Matthew 7:9-11 and compares it to God's method of giving:

Is there anyone here who, if his son asks him for a loaf of bread, will give him a stone? Or if he asks for a fish, will give him a snake? So if you, even though you are bad, know how to give your children gifts that are good, how much more will your Father in heaven keep giving good things to those who keep asking him!

Does God know how to give good gifts? Yes. Does God give evil gifts? No. Is the Law, given from God to His people an evil or a good gift? The answer should be obvious. Yet, by the attitude of many believers, it is as though the Law were evil. Oh, how they are missing the joy and liberty found within the Law God has given us!

Exodus 24: 12- 25:22; 34:28- 34:32; Leviticus 26:46, 27:34; Numbers 30:16; 36:13; Deuteronomy 4:13; 5:3 1; 33:2; 10:4; Psalms 147: 19; Nehemiah 9: 13,14

The Law is given to Israel to make them wise and understanding.

Deuteronomy 4:6-8

Abraham keeps God's Laws - What Laws? Where do we see God giving Laws to Abraham in the Bible? Yes, here we see God saying that Abraham kept His Laws, statutes and ordinances. True faith in God implies obedience to Him. Yes, Abraham's faith made him righteous, but his righteous faith caused him to obey God.

Genesis 26:5

God proves Israel to see if they will walk in His Laws - Just as He proved Abraham's faith in Him. Obedience to God's Law helps us to check out our true relationship with Him. If we love

Him, we will keep His commandments!

Exodus 16:4

One Law for Jew and Gentile - There was not a separate Law for Jews and Gentiles! There is only one Law for all believers! God did not want a special set of rules and regulations for the Hebrews and another set for the Gentile believers. Such a setup would have caused an exclusive attitude to have been built up in the community. Instead, both groups followed the same Law.

Exodus 12:49; Leviticus 18:26; 24:22; Numbers 15:16,29; 19: 10; Deuteronomy 31: 12

Same Law will judge the Nations - In fact, the same Law will be that which God uses to judge the unbelieving nations (Romans 2:14-16)! In other words, all the nations, even those who do not keep God's Laws, will one day be judged by them! This attests to the continuity of the Law as the standard of righteousness and holiness.

Isaiah 2:3; 42:4; 51:4

Law not to be changed - God does not want anyone to misrepresent Him, by adding to, or annulling, subtracting from, what He has said in His word. He wants His truth to be unadulterated and complete. Throughout history, abuses have occurred as a result of men changing the Word of God to suit their own needs. We do not have to go back too far to see David Koresh, Jim Jones, and others who misrepresented God's Word, often with fatal results. God therefore says of His Word: "Do not change it."

Deuteronomy 4:2

God wishes that His people would have such a heart in them that they would fear Him and keep all His commandments always. This passage to me always comes with a sigh from God. I could just imagine Him in the heavens looking down upon us and wishing that we would learn that His way is always right. If only we would keep it, it would go so much better for us!

Deuteronomy 5:29

Laws of Various offerings; laws of Sacrifice - Contained within the Law are various types of sacrifices. The sacrificial system was instituted to restore fellowship between man and God. Blood had to be shed to atone for sin so that man could come into God's presence. In the Millennial reign of Messiah, many of these sacrifices will be performed by the Levitical priesthood. The reason for this appears to be that during the Millennial reign the Messiah, God Incarnate, will reign and rule among sinful men. In a later chapter of this book (Chapter 6 - Taking it to the Wall), I will go into detail about this.

Exodus 29:8-28; Leviticus 6:9, 18, 22; 6:14; 7:1, 7, 11, 34-37; 10:9-15; 16:29-34; Numbers 6; 19:2; Joshua 8:31; 1 Chronicles 16:40; 2 Chronicles 8:13-15; 23:18; 30:16; 31:3; Nehemiah 10:34; 12:44

Law of Leprosy - the Law was set in place to protect God's people from disease. Allowing a contagious disease to run unchecked would have destroyed all of God's people, just as allowing sin to run unchecked will destroy us.

Leviticus 13:59; 14:2, 32, 54, 57

Kosher Laws - Wonder what is clean or unclean in God's eyes? These passages explain the Biblical kosher (clean) laws.

Exodus 30:21; Leviticus 11; Deuteronomy 14: 1 -22

Laws against Sexual Immorality. The other nations allowed for immorality that was not to be found among God's people. God here specifies what sexual practices are to be forbidden to His people.

Leviticus 18:15; 20: 12; Numbers 5:29; 27:23; Ezekiel 22: 11

Law Declared to the People - The Law was not given in a corner; it was published before all Israel at the mountain! This sets the method that God uses to give His Law. If the Law were to be changed or dispensed with altogether, shouldn't God let all the people of Israel know?

Numbers 31:21; Deuteronomy 1:5; 4:14,44,45; 5:1,31; 31:11, 12; 33:10; Joshua 8:34; 2 Kings 22:8, 11; 2 Chronicles 17:9; Ezra 7:6-26; 8:1-18; Nehemiah 9:3; Psalms 78:1,5; 94:12; 119: 1-21 26, 64, 68, 71, 124, 13 5, 17 1; Isaiah 1:10; 2:3

Not to Waver from the Judgment of the Law - God wanted to be sure that even the rulers of Israel be faithful to His Torah and not move either to the right or to the left.

Deuteronomy 17:18; Joshua 1:7; 23:6

Law Written - The commandments were not to be conveyed solely by oral means, lest something contrary creeps in over time. Instead, they were written so that they would be less likely to be misinterpreted or changed.

Deuteronomy 27:3, 8; 31:9; 31:24; Joshua 8:32; 24:26

The Law to be Kept - The preponderance of Scripture speaks of God's people keeping His Laws; not ignoring them, or flaunting a liberty apart from them.

Exodus 15:26; Leviticus 19:37; 20:8,22; 22:31; 23:14; 25:18; 26:3; Deuteronomy 4:5,6; 5:31; 6:125; 7:11; 8:1-11; 11: 1, 32; 12:1; 13: 4,18; 15:5; 26:16,17; 27:1-26; 28:1,9,58-61; 29:21; 30:8; 32:46, Joshua 22:5; 1 Kings 8:58, 61; 2 Kings 17:13-37; 18:6; 23:3, 24, 25; 1 Chronicles 22:12;2 Chronicles 6:16; 14:4; 19:10; 24:6; 29:19; 31:4; 34:31; Ezra 7:10; 10:3; Nehemiah 10:28,29,36; Psalm 1:2;78:7; 103:18 20; 119: 10, 19, 32, 34, 35, 44, 47, 48, 51, 55, 60, 61, 66, 73, 86, 96, 109, 115, 131, 143, 145,151,153,163,165,166,172, 176; Proverbs 3:1; 4:2; 6:23; 7:2; 28:7; Ecclesiastes 12:13; Isaiah 51:7; Ezekiel 11:12-20; 18:9; 36:27; 37:24; 44:24; Daniel 9:4; Zechariah 1:6

Sins of Ignorance, still guilty! - Just because you don't know something is a sin, it doesn't absolve you of your guilt if you violate God's commandment. Even in the world "Ignorance is no excuse" according to the law of the land. If you violate man's laws in ignorance and are held accountable, how much more so with God's?

Leviticus 4:2-27; 5:17

Law belongs to God's People forever. Everlasting Covenant — Examples of "forever" practices in the Old Testament - Does God have a problem understanding what forever means? I think not.

Leviticus 23:21,31,41;24:3,9; Numbers 18:11,19,23; 19:10,21; 35:29; Deuteronomy 29:29; 33:4; 1 Chronicles 16:17; Psalms 105:10

Law a Delight - What? You'd think from the attitude of some church people that it was pure bondage and enslavement...Are we talking about the same Law here, folks?

Psalms 119: 16, 70, 77, 92, 97,113, 174

Advantageous to Keep God's Laws - In many areas of our lives God's commandments are a benefit to us: in keeping us from disease, to making us secure, to keeping us fed and even to making us prosperous. It is to our advantage that we learn to obey His commandments and laws.

Exodus 15:26; 20:6; Leviticus 25:18; 26:3; Deuteronomy 4:1,40; 5:10,29; 6:2,24; 7:9; 10: 13; 11:8— 27; 28:13; 30:8-16; Joshua 1:8; 1 Samuel 12:14-15; 1 Kings 2:3; 3:14; 6:12; 11:34-38; 2 Kings 21:8; 1 Chronicles 22:13; 28:7-8; 2 Chronicles 31:21; 33:8; Nehemiah 1: 5-9; Psalms 19:8; 37:31; 112: 1; 119:6, 98; Proverbs 19:16; 29:18; Isaiah 48:18; Ezekiel 18:21; 20:11; 33:15

The Law of the Lord is Good; the Law is Truth - Since God is truth, this is a reflection of His nature.

Psalms 19:7; 119:142

Law to Stand as a Witness - When we do good, or when we do evil; the Law is the standard by which we judge the one from the other. The Law is not arbitrary or capricious. It is an eternal standard that will endure until the end of the ages. Unlike a judge in the human sense who can waver in judgement, the Law is unchanging, as God is unchanging.

Deuteronomy 31:26; 2 Kings 17:13-37; Nehemiah 9:16-34

Law Separates God's People From the World - God all along has called His people to be holy or separate from the world. If we obey His commandments, we will not be doing some of the things the world does.

Leviticus 18:26; Leviticus 19:19; Deuteronomy 26:17-18; 2 Kings 17:7-41; Ezra 9:14; Nehemiah 13:3; Psalms 119: 1,29; Ezekiel 11:12

Law Written in the Heart of God's People - He wants us to keep them so much that He didn't just leave them on tablets of stone. He wrote them on our hearts. This internalization allows us to keep them.

Exodus 13:9; Numbers 15:39,40; Psalms 40:8; Jeremiah 31:33; Psalms 119:23, 48, 80, 83, 112, 117; Malachi 4:4

Warnings for Those who Depart from God's Laws - Hear these words, brethren. You can't walk away from God's commandments and think that you will be ok. His commandments bless us; it's when we turn away from them that we are cursed.

Exodus 16:28; Leviticus 14:41; 26:15-16, 43; Numbers 15:22-31;Deuteronomy 11:28; 28:15-45; Joshua 1:18; Judges 2:17; 1 Samuel 15:24; 2 Samuel 12:9; 1 Kings 9:6; 11:33; 13:21; 14:8; 2 Kings 8:27; 10:31; 17:7-34;24:3; 2 Chronicles 7:19; 12:1; 15:3; 17:4; 24:21; Ezra 9:10-14; Nehemiah 9:26- 34; Psalm 78:10; 89:31; 119:21,53,85,118,126,13 6,155; Proverbs 13:13;19:16; 28:4,9; 31:5; Isaiah 5:24; 30:9;42:24; Jeremiah

2:8;6:19;8:8;9:13;16:11;26:4;32:23;44:10,13; Lamentations 1:18; 2:9; Ezekiel 5:6,7; 7:26; 20:13-25; 22:26; Daniel 9:11,13; Hosea 4:6; 8:1,12; Amos 2:4; Habakkuk 1:4; Zephaniah 3:4; Haggai 2:11; Zechariah 7:12; Malachi 2: 7-9

Law Shows Mercy and Compassion (Yes, there IS grace in the Law — we didn't have to wait until the Newer Testament to have that!) - Many take the passage in John 1:17 to mean that in the Older Testament there was no grace, but Law and in the Newer Testament there is no Law, but grace. This is not true. In both Testaments there is grace working together with Law.

Deuteronomy 26:13; 2 Kings 14:6; 2 Chronicles 25:4

Law Better than Gold or Silver - We should desire it more than gold or silver, for it speaks of the holiness of God and we should desire to be like Him.

Psalms 119:72

No Light in Those who speak not according to the Word - for those who say that the Law is done away with and not applicable in the lives of God's people today.

Isaiah 8:20

God will Magnify the Law and make it honorable - This is in the future, brethren. If the Law is to be disparaged, why will God magnify and honor it?

Isaiah 42:4

Law will go forth from Zion during Messianic Reign! - You would think that if Messiah fulfilled the law and dispensed with it that when He reigns on Zion, He wouldn't go back to it...

Micah 4:2

NEW TESTAMENT PASSAGES

Yeshua did NOT destroy or DO AWAY with the Law —

tells people to keep the Commandments - Yeshua (God Incarnate) lived a perfect life, obeying the commandments perfectly. We are to walk as he walked (1 John 2), therefore He was consistent in urging His followers to be obedient to the commandments.

Matthew 5: 17-19; 19:17; Mark 19:19; Luke 18:20

Yeshua fulfilled the Law which does not mean He abolished it. - "Fulfill" comes from the Old English word which means to fill full. If I were to fill a glass full of water, I would not suddenly see it vanish before my eyes when the water reached the top of the glass! Instead, I would see a glass full of water. When Yeshua fulfilled the Law, He perfectly obeyed it to its fulness! Yet, we do not see the law disappear as He filled it fully in the flesh. Instead, we have a flesh and blood example of how we are to walk.

Matthew 5:17; Luke 24:44; John 12:34; 15:25, Acts 28:23

Not one jot or tittle shall pass from the Law until heaven and earth pass - When will the Law be done away? You have your answer here. When I look around, I still see the earth and heavens...well, I guess the Law is still here, too.

Matthew 5:18; Luke 16:17

"Do Unto Others" is the Law and the Prophets - Some say Yeshua introduced new concepts in the New Testament. That is true, but the concept of "doing unto others" was found (per Yeshua) in the law and in the prophets.

Matthew 7:12

New Testament Observances of the Law - Did Yeshua and the Apostles observe the Law? Evidence is found in the New Testament that they did.

Luke 1: 6; 2:22-39; 23: 56; Acts 21:20-24; 22: 12; 24:14; 25: 8

Yeshua Versus the Pharisees' observance of the Law - The difference between Yeshuas' observance and the Pharisees' observance of the Law was one of motive. Why did Yeshua observe the Law? Out of love for the Father. Why did the Pharisees observe the law? To obtain their righteousness from it. The Law is not the issue here. The motive for keeping it is.

Matthew 15:3-9; 23; Mark 7:7-9; John 7:19-5 1; 8: 5

Law given by disposition of angels - As mentioned earlier, the Law is a gift from God to His people. It is given by a good God who gives good gifts, not evil gifts. The Law was not only given in a public forum on Sinai before all the people, it was also ordained by angels who looked on.

Acts 7: 53

Justification and righteousness through faith and not Law of Moses; Faith Versus Law.

Though justification and righteousness come only through faith and not through the Law of Moses, evidence that one is a true believer comes from obedience to God.

Acts 13 :39; Romans 3: 20-31; 4:13-16; 9:31-32; 10: 4-5; Galatians 2:16-21; 3: 2-24; 4: 4-21; 5:3-14; Philippians 3: 9

Law and Gentiles in New Testament - Does a Gentile have to keep the Law as depicted in the Older Testament? From the context of this passage, not for salvation. Of course, this is true for the Jew as well. No one is saved by keeping the Law. However, once saved, there is evidence that Moses becomes a part of their lives (Acts 15:21). Of what use is preaching Moses every Sabbath unless Moses has a value in the lives of believers?

Acts 15: 5-24

Sha'ul accused of subverting the Law - Were the accusations against Sha'ul true? If so, Sha'ul stands contrary to Yeshua in Matthew 5:17-19. It is evident from the Acts 21:17-28 passage that Sha'ul is establishing his faithfulness to the Law.

Acts 18: 13; 21: 17-26

Sin and Law - These passages in the Newer Covenant show us that the definition of sin comes from the Law. We could not know what sin is unless we had an objective standard to go by.

Romans 2: 12-27; 3:19; 5: 13, 20;6:14-15; 7:8-13; 8:2-7; 1 John 3: 4

Law has dominion over a person as long as he lives - as believers, when we die, we shall be with the Lord. Ultimately, we shall be in glorified, sinless bodies. In any event, we will be totally obedient to God. The Law won't be an external thing to us, it will actually become a part of our nature.

Romans 7: 1-25; 1 Corinthians 7: 39

LAW is GOOD, HOLY and JUST (the Apostle Sha'ul said this!)

Romans 7: 12; 1 Timothy 1: 8

Law is SPIRITUAL - The Law is not something we can fulfill through the strength of the flesh.Since it reflects God's nature, it is spiritual as He is Spirit.

Romans 7: 14

Law of Sin and Death - What is the law of sin and death? Is it the Law given at Sinai? Or is it something else?

Romans 8:2; 1 Corinthians 15:56

CARNAL mind is not subject to Law of God — Law not made for the righteous man. There are millions of laws on the books of mankind. We are obedient to most of them with little effort, since many of them are simply the result of righteous living. A righteous person will generally live a life in obedience to the laws of the land and will not get into trouble. There are those, however, who are rebellious and who desire to cause trouble. When they break the law, the punishment defined in the law will be given to them.

Romans 8:7; 1 Timothy 1:9

Law given to Israel - As mentioned earlier, the Law was a gift given to Israel. It was not an evil gift meant to enslave God's people in bondage, rather that if His people would keep His Laws, they would walk in prosperity and peace. Sha'ul confirms the giving of the Law here in this passage of the Newer Covenant.

Romans 9:4

Love is fulfilment of Law - Since God is love, it stands to reason that if one truly loves - he or she will be fulfilling God's Law.

John 13:34; Romans 13:8-10; Galatians 5:14; 6:2; 1 Timothy 1:5; James 2:8; 1 John 4:21; 5:2-3; 2 John 1:56

Sha'ul Quotes Law - If the Law has no value in the life of a believer, why quote it? If all Gentile believers had to do was found in Acts 15:20 and 29, why incorporate even 1 single verse to those verses? I submit, even Sha'ul brings Moses to the Gentiles (Acts 15:21) because they need to know what the standard of behavior is in their newfound community.

1 Corinthians 9:8-9; 14:21, 34

Sha'ul says he is not under the Law - I devote an extensive section to help a believer understand what Sha'ul is talking about. Obviously, it is not talking about being free from obedience to God's commandments, because he dispels that notion in Acts 21.

1 Corinthians 9:20, 21

Circumcision and Law - If Sha'ul is so set against circumcision, why does he have Timothy circumcised? Is he telling Jews not to have their children circumcised (Acts 21:21)? Not at all. In Corinthians and Galatians he is simply making the point that being circumcised does not justify a person.

Acts 15:24; Acts 21:21; 1 Corinthians 7:19; Galatians 5:3- 6

Yeshua abolishes in His flesh the enmity of the Law - The enmity of the Law comes because we cannot keep it (in the flesh). So saying, we would all be doomed were it not for the perfect sacrifice of Yeshua. This is not to say He abolished the Law, only the curse from us not keeping it.

Ephesians 2:15

Law and Priesthood - The two are inextricably entwined. Within the Law is found the definition of sin. The only remedy for sin is the sacrificial system and the only people allowed to offer the sacrifices were the cohanim (priests).

Hebrews 7:5-28; 9:19-22; 10: 1-23

Law of Liberty — compare with Psalm 119 - The way some believers view the Law, you would wonder: Are we talking about the same Law here? Is David in Psalm 119 a bit confused? Or are some church people who think the Law is bondage?

James 1:25; 2:12

Keep whole Law. Yet offend in one point — Guilty of all - This passage speaks to the legalists who seek to be justified through their keeping of the Law. If you are trying to obtain your righteousness by keeping the Law, you must keep it all, always. Anything short of that is sin and even one sin disqualifies you in your quest to obtain your righteousness by keeping the Law.

James 2: 10-12

If you love Me, keep My Commandments - Nothing has changed from the Older to the Newer Testaments, except the medium upon which the Law is written. The basis of our proof of love for Him is in our obedience to His commandments.

John 14:15-21; 15:10; 1John 5:2-3; 2 John 1:6, Revelation 22:1

How do you KNOW that you KNOW Him? If you KEEP His Commandments - You show your relationship with Him through your obedience. If you live a life in disobedience to His commandments, you should question whether you have a true relationship with Him at all.

1 John 2:3-8; 3:22-24; 5:2- Revelation 12:17; 14:12; 22:14

These and many more passages from the Scripture establish the continuance and the necessity of the Law in the lives of God's people. Far from abolishing the Law, they *establish* the Law. By denying the applicability of the Law in the lives of Christians, many theologians and pastors deny the blessings inherent in keeping the Laws of God to their fellow believers. There are blessings given to God's people as a result of keeping His Laws and much spiritual truth that can be learned by experiencing His word!

Chapter 5

THE PURPOSE OF THE LAW

I believe there are three basic purposes of the Law and why it was given:

1 - for our *own good* (Deuteronomy 6:24; 17-19)

2 - to show us the holiness of God (Romans 7:12; Leviticus 11: 44) and what sin is (Romans 7:7)

3 - to lead us to Messiah that we may be justified by faith (Galatians 3:24) The Law was given for our own good, - and not by a God who desired to "squish" His people into a dull, boring lifestyle by forcing them to submit to unjust, unwanted laws.

The Law is **"good, holy and just"** (Romans 7:12). In it we find **"wisdom"** (Psalm 119: 98), **"grace"** (Psalms 119: 124) and **"liberty"** (Psalm 119:45). It is a gift for mankind (Romans 9:4), and should be regarded in the light of James 1:17, 18, 21-25:

Every good act of giving and every perfect gift is from above, coming down from the Father who made the heavenly lights; with him there is neither variation nor darkness caused by turning. Having made his decision, he gave birth to us through a Word that can be relied upon, in order that we should be a kind of firstfruits of all that he created. So rid yourselves of all vulgarity and obvious evil, and receive meekly the Word implanted in you that can save your lives. Don't deceive yourselves by only hearing what the Word says, but do it! For whoever hears the Word but doesn't do what it says is like someone who looks at his face in a mirror, who looks at himself, goes away and immediately for-

gets what he looks like. But if a person looks closely into the perfect Torah, which gives freedom, and continues, becoming not a forgetful hearer but a doer of the work it requires, then he will be blessed in what he does.

Since the Law is considered a gift to mankind, the question must be asked, "Does God give bad gifts?"

Is there anyone here who, if his son asks him for a loaf of bread, will give him a stone? Or if he asks for a fish, will give him a snake? So if you, even though you are bad, know how to give your children gifts that are good, how much more will your Father in heaven keep giving good things to those who keep asking him! (Matthew 7:9-11).

The Father, who loves us all, knows what is good for us, and He gave us the Torah! It was given for our own good (Deuteronomy 6:25), not to bind us in legalism. Since we are made in the image of God, we should want to be holy as He is! The Law, being a reflection of God's holiness, acts as a mirror to us. When we look into the mirror of the Law and look at ourselves, we find truly that we all **"fall short of the glory of God."**

At this point the separation between the hearers and the doers of the Word becomes evident. The one who is a hearer only looks at himself through the Law and says, "Well who can reach it?" and walks away doing nothing to change himself. The doer looks at the same Law and says, "Woe is me, I am a man of unclean lips," then seeks God's strength in wanting to live a holy life and to keep God's Laws. Without God's strength, it is impossible to live a holy life.

As noted in the preceding Chapter, the Law is perfect; yet, there was a need for a New Covenant.

The Book of Hebrews notes this in Chapter 8:

Indeed, if the first covenant had not given ground for fault-finding, there would have been no need for a second one.

(verse 7).

There *was* a fault with the first covenant; — not in it's conveyance for God delivered it Himself (Deuteronomy 5:22), writing it with His own finger. It was not in the commandments, for they reflect His holiness. **"Be yourselves holy, for I am holy** (Leviticus 11:45- NASB). No, the fault lies elsewhere:

For God does find fault with the people when he says, "See! The days are coming," says Adonai, "when I will establish over the house of Isra'el and over the house of Y'hudah a new covenant. It will not be like the covenant which I made with their fathers on the day when I took them out by their hand and led them forth out of Egypt; because they, for their part, did not remain faithful to my covenant; so I, for my part, stopped concerning myself with them," says Adonai. (Hebrews 8:8,9)

The fault of the Law was in the people's inability to keep it. That is why God did not care for them! They did not keep His Law! So, He remedies this by making a New Covenant with the house of Israel and Judah.

If you note carefully in the New Testament, there are *no* new Laws to those found in the Old Testament (although Yeshua expanded on the Law of Moses in His Sermon on the Mount); instead, there is the power through the Holy Spirit to keep the already-given laws of God:

For this is the covenant which I will make with the house of Isra'el after those days, says Adonai: I will put My Torah in their minds, and will write it on their hearts (Hebrews 8: 10).

God doesn't say He'll Write new Laws, rather that He'll write His Laws upon the minds and hearts of His people, so that they will do them!

I will give you a new heart and put a new spirit inside you; I will take the stony heart out of your flesh and give you a

heart of flesh. I will put my Spirit inside you and cause you to live by my laws, respect my rulings and obey them. (Ezekiel 36:26,27)

God wants us to keep His commandments, because it shows our love for Him!

Oh, how I wish their hearts would stay like this always, that they would fear me and obey all my mitzvot; so that it would go well with them and their children forever. (Deuteronomy 5:29).

No, the commandments were not given by an angry God who wanted to enslave His people by a bunch of unwanted laws! Instead, they were given by a loving God who wants to be loved, and wants the best for His children.

Why does a parent say to a small child, "Don't touch the stove! Is it so the poor little thing can feel the repression of a domineering parent who likes to throw his weight around simply because he is bigger than the child? No, it is because the parent loves the child and wants the best for that child, not wishing to see him hurt.

God wants the same for us. He gave us His Laws so that we would have a means to express our love for Him. Our lip service isn't enough. If all we had to do was to praise God with our lips in word and song to show our love for God, then why did Yeshua criticize the Pharisees?

You hypocrites! Yesha'yahu was right when he prophesied about you, "These people honor me with their lips, but their hearts are far from me. Their worship of me is useless, because they teach man-made rules as if they were doctrines." (Matthew 15:7,8)

One's heart is not reflected only through words, but through action, living a holy life God has called us to live because in doing so, we show our love to God.

Here is how we know that we love God's children: when we love God, we also do what he commands. For loving God means obeying his commands. Moreover, his commands are not burdensome... (1 John 5:2,3).

Not only, then, is it a *benefit* for us to keep His commandments, but it is also a reflection of our love for God. If that is the case, why does the Body of Messiah look with such disdain upon those who keep it?

I see the Jewish people and their respect and love for the Torah of God, and then I look at the Body of Messiah with its disdain for that same Torah. Why is this so? I believe it is because the Scriptures have somehow gotten twisted in Platonic (Greek) thought, and the Hebrew concepts have somehow "gotten lost in the translation."

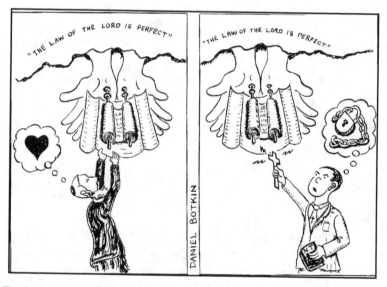

Early on, the Church uprooted itself from its Jewish roots and incorporated within its theology a Greek outlook (world view). Hebrew notes that "faith"(Hebrew: emoonah) is not only cognitive (reasoned), but also active (manifested in a life) whereas, the Greek isolates the cognitive from its resulting action. A Greek could "believe" in God yet live a life far apart from what

God wants. James 2:19 gives us an example of Greek reasoning.. Ya'akov tells us demons believe in God, yet don't live lives reflecting what God wants, hence, they tremble.

Some Christians live lives with this type of thinking. They'll go to church on Sunday, and live lives contrary to God's will the rest of the week. This is in opposition to Hebraic thinking where Abram **"believed in the Lord and He** (God) **reckoned it to him as righteousness"** (Genesis 15:5-NASB).**Yet "Abraham obeyed Me** (God) **and kept My** (His) **charge, My** (His) **commandments, My** (His) **statutes and My** (His) **Laws."** (Genesis 26:5-NASB)

The dynamic between faith and works becomes evident in Hebrew thought; whereas, this same dynamic can be isolated in Greek thought as James illustrates in Chapter 2: 14-17:

What good is it, my brothers, if someone claims to have faith but has no actions to prove it? Is such "faith" able to save him? Suppose a brother or sister is without clothes and daily food, and someone says to him, "Shalom! Keep warm and eat hearty!" Without giving him what he needs, what good does it do? Thus, faith by itself, unaccompanied by actions, is dead.

In effect, if you have a true faith, you will have resulting works — obedience being one of them. If you truly know Him, you *will* obey His commandments. How can you know that you truly know Him?

The way we can be sure we know him is if we are obeying his commandments. Anyone who says, "I know him," but doesn't obey his commands is a liar the truth is not in him. But if someone does what he says, then truly the love for God has been brought to its goal in him.This is how we can be sure we are united with him. A person who claims to be continuing in union with him ought to conduct his life the way he did. Dear friends, I am not writing you a new com-

mand. On the contrary, it is an old command, which you have had from the beginning; the old command is the message you have heard before. (1 John 2:3-7).

In other words, a believer in Yeshua should walk just as He (Yeshua) walked while He was on this earth. Not flaunting a freedom apart from the Law, but rather exhibiting a freedom found within the Law. Yeshua lived what David wrote about in Psalm 119. Obeying God's Laws perfectly, Yeshua showed what a Spirit-filled believer in God should be doing: living in obedience to God's Laws.

When the Giver of the Law indwells the heart of the believer, He empowers that believer to live in accordance with the Law. By being obedient to the Law, the believer then exhibits the love of God in his or her life towards God and his fellow-man.

Chapter 6

TAKING IT TO THE WALL

Taking our theology "to the wall" means that we take a doctrine and follow it to its logical conclusion.

As I explained in the preceding chapters, I believe the Body of Messiah has compromised its position of being obedient to God's commandments resulting in moral relativism in today's world. If such is true, and the Christian position as relates to the Law leads to a moral relativism, then what does the position contained herein lead?

Since the Law contains the sacrificial system, it follows that one day if the Law is re-instituted the sacrificial system will resume. The logical conclusion of obedience to the Law is to a resumption of the sacrificial system, since that is an integral part of the Law.

To most Christians this would seem unthinkable! It would be argued at since Yeshua was the ultimate sacrifice; no longer is there a need for a sacrificial system for believers. However, that is not necessarily true; if it were why then did Sha'ul (as a believer) offer a sacrifice to show his obedience to the Law in Acts 21:15-26 (see also Numbers 6) at the bequest of the other believing disciples?

It is a point of fact that during the Millennium when Yeshua reigns there will be the restoration of the Levitical sacrifices (Jeremiah 33:14-22; Ezekiel 43 and 44). If the Levitical sacrifices were not needed, why does Yeshua allow them during His physical reign on this earth? It seems inconceivable that if the Old Testament Law were so negative that God would once again restore the Levitical system! Why restore something that didn't work?

The Book of Hebrews is very clear that the sacrificial system of the Law is not enough to take away sins (Hebrews 10: 1-9) and that Yeshua's blood is the only thing that is capable of doing so. Wouldn't the resumption of the sacrificial system seem to indicate that Yeshua' blood isn't enough? So, why will the sacrificial system be resumed in the Messianic reign of Yeshua on the earth? When Yeshua reigns on earth, can't He just say,"Don't you know, you Levitical priests, that My blood atoned for all sin and you don't need to do that stuff anymore?"

Of course He could; yet, the Bible is clear that in that day the Levitical priesthood will be restored, and that the Levitical sacrifices will resume (Jeremiah 33:15-22)!

What types of offerings will they offer? Ezekiel 40:38-32; 43:13-17; 44:28-31; 45:13-25; 46: 1-24 depicts that there will be burnt offerings. There will be guilt offerings as found in chapters 40:38- 43;43:13-17 and 46: 1-24. The cereal or grain offering described in chapter 44:28-31, as well as the offerings of first fruits are also performed at this time. We see the free will offering in chapter 44:28- 31 and 46:1-24. The peace offering is found in chapter 45:13-25 and 46:1-24, and the drink offering is found in chapter 45:13-25.

From these verses, it is clear that the sacrificial system did not end with the death and resurrection of Yeshua—neither in the past (up until the destruction of the Temple in C.E. 70), nor in the future (in the Messianic reign) when the Temple will once again be built.

We see many Biblical references to a third Temple: Ezekiel 37:26-28; Ezekiel 40-48 (specifically 43:1,2); Joel 3: 18; Amos 9:11; Micah 4:1,2; Zechariah 6:13 -15; 14:21; Malachi 3:1,2; Matthew 24:15; 2 Thessalonians 2:2-12; Revelation 11:1-3; Daniel 9:24-26; and Daniel 12:8-12.

When will the third Temple be built? Even now as of this writing, the priesthood in Israel is being trained to perform the sacrificial system. The implements have been crafted with meticulous detail, and all is being made ready. Though the Bible does not specifically state exactly when the Temple will be built, we do know this: it will be built *before* Yeshua returns.

Micah 4:1,2 says it will be in the last days that the mountain of the house of the Lord will be established. Malachi 3:1,2 says that the Lord will suddenly come to His Temple and you can't go to something that doesn't exist!

In Matthew 24:15; 2 Thessalonians 2:2-12; Revelation 11:1-3; Daniel 9:24-26 and Daniel 12:8-12 it is evident that the Temple will likely be constructed prior to the last 3 1/2years of the Great Tribulation, for the sacrifices are already instituted and the Anti-Messiah sets himself up in the Temple.

This third Temple will be the Messiah's seat of power and rule during the Millennium as seen in Micah 4:1,2; Zechariah 6:13-15 and Isaiah 60:13. It will also be the place of sacrifice: Ezekiel chapters 40- 48; Isaiah 62:12; Zechariah 14:21; Daniel 9: 24-26; and Daniel 12:8-12. Most importantly, it will be Messiah's dwelling place among men in Ezekiel chapters 40-48 and specifically chapter 43:1-5.

Lastly, the rebuilt Temple will be a sign to the world of Israel's sanctification: Ezekiel 37:26-28.

The Biblical references to a future priesthood are found in Isaiah 66:21-24; Jeremiah 31:14; 33:22; Ezekiel 40:44-47; 42:13,14; 43:19;44:9-31; 45: 1-5; 46:19-24; 48:8-22; 12:13; and Malachi 3:1-5.

Even when Yeshua walked on the earth, though He denounced abuses in the Temple and prophecied its destruction, He never repudiated the Temple services. He came to Jerusalem for the great Jewish feasts, and after His crucifixion and resurrection, His disciples still made their way to the Temple at the hour of prayer (Acts 3) and Sha'ul even offered the sacrifices of a Nazirite! (Numbers 6:13-20 cf. Acts 21:26).

In the end the Messiah will reign, and the Temple services will resume. This indicates that the Mosaic Law is not over yet, and serious truth seekers must rethink what the theologians have fed them over the years.

The Book of Hebrews, written about 69 A.D. speaks on the issue of the transition of the older to the newer covenants. It says, **"By using the term, 'new,' he has made the first covenant 'old'; and something being made old, something in the process of aging, is on its way to vanishing altogether"** (Hebrews 8, verse 13). This means that the Old Covenant had not disappeared even by 69 A.D, approximately thirty years after the death and resurrection of Yeshua. Instead, there is a transition period between the two covenants where one gradually disappears and the other replaces the older.

Technically speaking, we are not yet in the New Covenant period, even as you read this! We are still in the transition period depicted here in Hebrews 8:13! Why do I say this? Because God is specific about the characteristics of the New Covenant period. He says:

"For this is the covenant which I will make with the house of Isra'el after those days," says Adonai: "I will put my Torah in their minds and write it on their hearts; I will be their God, and they shall be my people. None of them will teach his fellow-citizen or his brother, saying, 'Know Adonai!' FOR ALL WILL KNOW ME, FROM THE LEAST OF THEM TO THE GREATEST, because I will be merciful toward their wickedness and remember their sins no more." [Capitals mine] (Hebrews 8:10-11).

We will know that we are in the New Covenant period when *everyone* knows the Lord. At that time we won't need synagogues, or churches; we won't need Bible studies, or Bible teachers; we won't need rabbis, or pastors, or priests to teach us about God, for we will all know God personally.

Until that time, we are *not* in the New Testament period in its fullness; we are *still in transition* - further evidence that the Laws of God are *still* in effect.

When, then, will the New Testament period come into it's fullness? I believe that the phrase, **"And I will be their God and they shall be My people"** points to when this time will be.

Jeremiah 31:33; 33:38; Ezekiel 11:20; 36:28; Hebrews 8:10, and others speak of *a future* time when the Laws of God will be within us and we will walk in total obedience to them. It is obvious that we are not in that time now, especially considering the current rebelliousness and/or ignorance of many of God's people toward His Laws.

I personally believe that this time will be found in Revelation 21, with the bringing forth of the new heavens and earth and the doing away of the first heaven and earth (verse 1). This points to a time when **"he will live with them. They will be his peoples, and he, himself, God-with-them, will be their God** (verse 3).

This truly will be a time when all people will know Him from the least to the greatest and we will not need anyone to teach us about God. It is at this time that the New Covenant in its fullness will explode and the old will be totally done away.

CHAPTER 7

Sha'ul and the LAW: Liar, Hypocrite, "Least in Kingdom of Heaven," or Misunderstood?

As alluded to in Chapter 4 of this book, the anti-Nomian (anti-Law) bias in the Body of Messiah stems mostly from the Apostle Sha'ul's writings on the subject. As also noted in this chapter, the majority position of the Biblical Scriptures as pertaining to God's commandments, statutes and laws speak of keeping them.

Yet, passages in Sha'ul's writings seem to lend themselves themselves to the interpretation of being against the keeping of God's Laws. For the purposes of accurately reflecting contemporary Christian teaching on the subject, I will quote in this chapter from the New American Standard Version of the Bible:

"For sin shall not be master over you, for you are not under law, but under grace" (Romans 6:14),

"Therefore, my brethren, you also were made to die to the Law through the body of Christ, that you might be joined to another, to Him who was raised from the dead, that we might bear fruit for God" (Romans 7:4)

"For the law of the Spirit of life in Christ Jesus has set you free from the law of sin and of death" (Romans 8:2)

"And to the Jews I became as a Jew, that I might win Jews; to those who are under the Law, as under the Law, though not being myself under the Law, that I might win those who are under the Law; to those who are without law, as with-

out law, though not being without the law of God but under the law of Christ, that I might win those who are without law" (1 Corinthians 9:20-21)

"For Christ is the end of the law for righteousness to everyone who believes" (Romans 10:4)

"All things are lawful, but not all things edify" (1 Corinthians 10:23)

"Now the Lord is Spirit; and where the Spirit of the Lord is, there is liberty" (2 Corinthians 3:17),

"Nevertheless, knowing that a man is not justified by the works of the Law but through faith in Christ Jesus, even we have believed in Christ Jesus, that we may be justified by faith in Christ, and not by the works of the Law; since by the works of the Law shall no flesh be justified" (Galatians 2:16)

"This is the only thing I want to find out from you: did you receive the Spirit by the works of the Law, or by hearing with faith? Are you so foolish? Having begun by the Spirit, are you now being perfected by the flesh? Did you suffer so many things in vain if indeed it was in vain? Does He, who provides you with the Spirit and works miracles among you, do it by the works of the Law, or by hearing with faith?" (Galatians 3:2-5),

"Therefore the Law has become our tutor to lead us to Christ, that we may be justified by faith. But now that faith has come, we are no longer under a tutor. For you are all sons of God through faith in Christ Jesus" (Galatians 3:24-26)

"Tell me, you who want to be under law, do you not listen to the law?" (Galatians 4:21)

"But if you are led by the Spirit, you are not under the Law" (Galatians 5:18),

"But the fruit of the Spirit is love, joy, peace, patience, kindness, goodness, faithfulness, gentleness, self-control; against such things there is no law" (Galatians 5:22,23),

"For by grace you have been saved through faith; and that not of yourselves, it is the gift of God; not as a result of works that no one should boast" (Ephesians 2: 8,9),

"For He Himself is our peace, who made both groups into one, and broke down the barrier of the dividing wall, by abolishing in His flesh the enmity which is the Law of commandments contained in ordinances, that in Himself He might make the two into one man, thus establishing peace, and might reconcile them both in one body to God through the cross, by having put to death the enmity" (Ephesians 2:14-16),

"But we know that the Law is good, if one uses it lawfully, realizing the fact that the Law is not made for a righteous man, but for those who are lawless and rebellious, for the ungodly and sinners, for the unholy and profane, for those who kill their fathers or mothers, for murderers and immoral men and homosexuals and kidnappers and liars and perjurers, and whatever else is contrary to sound teaching according to the glorious gospel of the blessed God, with which I have been entrusted" (1 Timothy1:8-11).

As we read these passages and others like them we can see how easy it is to put together a theology that speaks of **"the end of the Law," "law of sin and death," "law of bondage,"** etc. The question is, what is the real message Sha'ul intends to convey?

The reason I pose this question is because his actions seem to speak of something else. For instance, in the 1 Corinthians 9:20 account, Sha'ul portrays himself as, **"not being myself under the Law..."** A similar vein extends from himself to believers in Galatians 5:18 when he says, " **if you are led by the Spirit,**

you are not under the Law," and the Romans 14:14 passage which says, **"For sin shall not be master over you, for you are not under law, but under grace."** It would seem, then, that not only he but *all* believers are exempt from following the commandments of the Law.

His actions in Acts 21:19-26 speak otherwise, however. As proof to the **"zealous"** Jews for the Law, and to the other Disciples, he carries out the Nazirite vow (Numbers 6) to make a statement that he **"walks orderly, keeping the Law."**

Other passages indicate his obedience to the Law, as well. In Acts 20: 16, Sha'ul is in a hurry to get to Jerusalem on Pentecost—in obedience to Exodus 23: 16 and Deuteronomy 16:10. Observing the Feast of Unleavened Bread – in obedience to Exodus 23:15, the **"fast"** of Yom Kippur in Acts 27:9 — in obedience to Leviticus 16:3 1, and other examples of faithfulness such as observing the Jewish Sabbath in Acts 13:14, 44; 16:13; 17:1,2,10,17; 18:7,8.

How can we reconcile Sha'ul's **"keeping the Law"** with his statements seemingly contrary to the Law? Is Sha'ul a "people-pleaser" or a chameleon?

As brought out in the title of this chapter, several possibilities exist. The first two are obvious: lying and hypocrisy. What do we call a person who says one thing and yet does the opposite? Of course, we call him a hypocrite! Considering that he stood up to Kefa for his hypocrisy in Galatians 2:11-15, I would call him worse than a hypocrite if what appears on the surface is true. Hypocrisy is the same as lying, and that's a sin. I seriously doubt that Sha'ul would stoop that low as he shared the Gospel.

Another option is perhaps in spreading the Gospel, he was annulling the Law and so teaching others.However, that would subject him to the Matthew 5:19 injunction and place him as **"least in the kingdom of heaven,"** according to Yeshua! However, knowing of Sha'ul's desire finish the race, so as to win the **"upward call of Christ"** (Philippians 3:14), I can't imagine Sha'ul deliberately wishing to violate Yeshuas' injunction and seeking to be **"least in the kingdom of heaven."**

This leaves us with one other option, and the most likely: Perhaps he has been misunderstood; perhaps it is possible to be obedient and keep the Law, while not being **"under the Law."**

Therefore, when Sha'ul speaks of being "hupo nomos"- **"under the law,"** is he speaking of legalism or obedience to the Laws and commandments of God because of a love relationship with Him? There is a big distinction here, yet no way to differentiate between them in Koine Greek. This is the danger of solely using Sha'ul's writings to justify the flaunting, negating or ignoring of the Law of God.

Furthermore, an additional area of misunderstanding Sha'ul's writings exists: Since in the Jewish mind there is a written Law and an Oral Law, could Sha'ul be speaking disparagingly about the Oral Law versus the Written Law? Remember, Yeshua experienced the same difficulty with the Pharisees regarding the Sabbath observance in the Gospel accounts. Yeshua had a problem not with the Written Law, but with the Oral Law! Hence, the negativism of being **"under the Law "** could likely be referencing a legalistic observance of the Law in order to obtain justification by it or it could be relative to the burdens of the Oral Law.

In this book I am bringing up various other possibilities than those taught by the leaders in the church throughout the centuries so that you, the reader, be you Christian or Jew, will see the need to seek out the truth for yourself. (And, to be fair, Jewish teaching has been wrong before, and we need to reject that which is contrary to God's Word anywhere we find it.) In so doing we will be like the Bereans in Acts 17: 10,11 who examined what Sha'ul said the standard of the Old Testament to see if what was said by Sha'ul was true.

It is possible to understand Sha'ul 's perspective and harmonize it with the Law of God from an Hebrew perspective. By so doing we will understand that Sha'ul was neither a hypocrite, liar, nor **"least in the kingdom of heaven."** Not only does he keep the Law himself, but he also quotes from it for the Gentiles in his writings. In short, he is an orthodox, believing Jew desiring all people to realize that salvation is by faith alone, not through the keeping of the Law.

The Law then becomes our tutor which leads us to the conclusion that righteousness can only come through faith, since it is impossible to keep all the Law always. Are we to forget the teachings of the tutor once we graduate from school? No, what foolishness!

Many of us have spent thousands and thousands of dollars on a college education. Are we going to say, "Now that I have graduated and received my degree, I don't need any of the stuff I learned from my professors. That stuff just doesn't apply to my life anymore"?

No. Hardly. We still need the information we received from the professors; we just don't need the professors anymore. The same holds true for the Law. The lessons are pertinent and necessary for us to live godly lives; the Law just doesn't have to keep teaching us the lessons once we've learned them! We are to take what we learned from our tutor and use it as a basis in our lives. This what the Law does in the lives of God's people. The tutor leads us to what is right and away from what is wrong. Once we learn these lessons, we no longer need the tutor to lead us.

Once we learn how to lead righteous lives in obedience to God, we no longer need the Law for instruction, because we will have teamed the lessons pertaining to righteousness and will do what the Law required. This is the real nature of the New Covenant.

Chapter 8

ONE LAW FOR ALL

There will be some believers who will concede at this point that the Law is still valid, but only for the Jew who has put himself or herself **"under the Law."**

The Scripture, however, paints a different picture. The Law given at Sinai was given to Jews and to **"sojourners"** (Hebrew: "gerim" - Gentiles who left Egypt along with the Israelites and attached themselves to the Hebrew people) —eventually to be known as "converts" or "proselytes," Exodus 12:49; Leviticus 24:22; Numbers 15:14-16). Anyone who joined themselves to Israel was subject to the same Law, and since Gentile believers are grafted into Israel (Romans 11), they technically are **"sojourners."**

Acts 15 says that Gentiles are to **"abstain from things polluted by idols, from fornication, from what is strangled and from blood."** But that does not mean that is all that is Gentile believer will have to follow. Verse 21 of that chapter also states that Moses is preached in the synagogue where, by the way, the early Gentile believers went (Acts 17:4, 17; 18:1-4) every Sabbath. There were no Catholics, Methodists, Baptists or other denominations at that time. This means that since Gentile believers (sojourners) were there, they heard Moses speak through Torah and learned what it meant to be holy.

The question answered in Acts 15 is this– Do Gentiles have to first become Jews —observing the Laws of Moses – before they can be saved? The answer is a resounding, "NO!" Rather, Gentiles are to follow the principles of an earlier covenant than the covenant given at Mount Sinai. Once they are saved, they are to follow the covenant God made with mankind through Noah, known as the Noachide Laws (Genesis 9).

This is not to say that Gentiles are not required to learn from the complete Word, which at that time was solely the Hebrew Scriptures of the Old Testament, so that they can move from a paganistic state of life to a holy life. The implication of Acts 15: 21 is that since Moses (the Law) is read every Sabbath in the synagogue, and since believing Gentiles had nowhere else to study the Word but the synagogue, they would hear the Law and begin to apply its principles in their lives. How far they went depended upon them and their relationship with God.

It is obvious from Acts Chapter 10 that Cornelius, the first convert in the believing community of Messiah, observed many Jewish customs and practices in his life. He gave many alms to the Jewish people, and he prayed continually. Verse 2 says he was a devout man, a **"God-fearer."**

The **"God-fearers,"** as they were known, identified with the Jewish faith, but did not necessarily subject themselves to circumcision (which was a requirement should a male choose to join himself totally as a convert to Judaism).

What makes Acts 10 interesting is verse 3, where Cornelius was praying at the ninth hour of the day.This was the time of the Temple sacrifice, and currently is the time when Jews pray in memorial to the sacrificial offering of the Temple. In other words, Cornelius was doing a very Jewish thing, yet he was not Jewish. God never stopped a Gentile from observing Jewish things, nor, by the way, from going all the way into Judaism.

If the Acts 15 injunction were all there was for the Gentile believer to observe, why did Sha'ul put even one single verse of the Torah, the Writings, or the Prophets in any of his writings to the Gentiles? For instance, in Romans 4:3 he cites Genesis 15:6; in Romans 3:10 he cites Psalm 53:3; in Romans 11:26 he cites Isaiah 59:20; in I Corinthians 9:9 he cites Deuteronomy 25:4; in 1 Corinthians 15:32 he quotes Isaiah 22:13;.in 1 Corinthians 3:20 he cites Psalm 94:11. Get the point? If *all* a

Gentile believer had to do was found in Acts 15, he or she wouldn't need to know or do anything more.

But just as Ruth, the Moabitess said to Naomi, **"Your people shall be my people and your God shall be my God"** (Ruth 1: 16); so Gentiles throughout the centuries have joined themselves to the people of God, worshiping Him as He desires to be worshiped, keeping His commandments alongside the Jewish people. God especially blesses the full convert to Judaism saving him separately from the **"God-fearer"** like Cornelius in the first outpouring of the Holy Spirit on Shavuot, or Pentecost (Acts 2:10). The full proselytes (alongside full-blooded, believing Jews) were baptized with the Spirit a full 10 years *before* Cornelius and others like him.

It is important to remember here that the intention of the Law was never to make one righteous (hence the sacrificial system). Instead, its teaching was two-fold: *it taught how one became a part of the covenant community of God through grace* (Deuteronomy 7:7-9; cf Ephesians 2:8-9) and *how a person was to behave within this covenant community.*

Even the New Testament teaches that we were created for **"good works"** (Ephesians 2:10) what standard did they go by (remembering that no New Testament" was available at the time)? Of course, it was the standard found within the Law.

Both Jew and Gentile alike are brought into covenant community by grace alone and not works, yet, it is through a person's obedience the commandments found within the covenant that he proves he is a part of the covenant community. How many commandments a covenant person keeps or ignores does not make him more or less righteous than another covenant person. It is by faith *alone* that righteousness is imputed (Genesis 15:6; cf Romans 4:3,9; Galatians 3:6; James 2:23).

The Jew is made righteous by the same standard as the full-proselyte and non-convert: by the standard of faith found in Romans 9:30-33. Yet, obedience to God's commandments is *assumed* of the faithful (Genesis 26:5; cf James 2:14-26). A Jew should be more faithful to God's commandments than the non-Jew (both full and non-proselyte), having been raised with the commandments. A full-proselyte should be more faithful than the non-proselyte, having learned more about how a covenant person is to behave. All should be desirous of being faithful to God's commandments due to a sense of gratitude and love for Him (Deuteronomy 10: 12-13). All should desire to move from a less holy behavior to a more holy behavior. This can only be accomplished by following God's commandments as laid out in the whole Bible.

CHAPTER 9

Please Don't Touch My Food!

Whenever one talks about food, one talks about something very personal to an individual, and the Biblical Laws of kashruit (kosher) seem to touch a particularly sensitive nerve with many Christians. Raised to believe that "anything goes" as pertains to what a person eats, many get very aggressive when confronted with God's Laws relative to what can or cannot be eaten.

"Well, Jesus pronounced all foods clean in-Mark 7:19, so we can eat anything we like. Or, "Kefa's vision in Acts 10 is God's way of saying that the kashruit laws are no longer valid." Or, God says, "What God has cleansed, no longer consider unholy."

It is possible to come to this understanding. Obviously so, because many believe this, but only because they take these passages out of context. I often listen to Dr. Woodrow Kroll, on *"BACK TO THE BIBLE"* on the radio. While I do not necessarily come to the same conclusion as he does relative to many Biblical issues, I find his teachings on Biblical interpretation to be quite sound. I'd like to share two of them with you:

First: **"When a passage in the Bible makes sense, seek no other sense."** In other words, if we read a Bible passage and within the context of the passage a clear understanding of what is being talked about exists, then don't try to carry it to another step. Too often people try to find "hidden meanings" in the Scripture and spiritualize passages that clearly speak to an issue. When they do this, they often come with the wackiest theology. No, the best way to interpret Scripture is to keep that passage in the context of the whole and let the Bible speak for itself.

Second: **"Never interpret a passage in the Bible in a way that conflicts with the rest of the Bible."** If the Bible has already in several ways spoken clearly to an issue and you find passage that seems to contradict what was clearly taught in the other passages, then go with what the majority of the Bible says. Sometimes when something seems contradictory it is because of translation difficulties. Sometimes, it is because the character or writer has his or her own viewpoint that conflicts with God's perspective in the rest of His Word. Sometimes, it is because we haven't followed rule number one as laid out here. Usually there is a good explanation, and we need to go back to the original language or to the character and find out what is really being said. In NO case should we change the Biblical position on account of one passage.

The late Dr. Walter Martin, founder of the Christian Research Institute in Southern California, hammered into his listeners this rule: **"Text, without context, is pretext."** Always, always keep the passage in the context of what is being said before and after that passage. If you take a text out of its context, you will come out with faulty theology virtually every time.

For instance, the Scripture says: **"and (Judas) went away and hanged** himself (Matthew 27:5); **"and Jesus said, Go and do the same"** (Luke 10:37). By tying these two unrelated passages together out of their context, we arrive at the conclusion that Yeshua is exhorting us (or someone) to go out and hang ourselves just as Judas did.

It is kind of ridiculous, isn't it? Yet, we are willing to do *exactly* that when it comes to other matters in Scripture; *especially* when it comes to the sensitive topic of Biblical kashruit. Citing several passages from various parts of the Bible out of their context, the church has come up with the theology that just as the Law has no place in the life of a believer, so, too, Biblical kashruit, a part of that Law, has no place in the life of a believer.

Let's first establish our groundwork: In the Torah a Biblical kashruit was laid out. Leviticus 11 and Deuteronomy 14:1-20 specifically state what foods are to be eaten and what things are not to be eaten.

In the Hebrew mind, what God has pronounced "clean" is classified "food." Nothing outside of that category is considered "food:" bats are not considered "food;" centipedes, bees, snakes, ravens, eagles, vultures, eels, squid, octopus, shrimp, lobster, clams, crabs, or people (for the cannibals out there), are not considered "food.." In short, the Hebrew mind says that anything God said was unclean simply is not categorized as "food."

 It is implied, though not specified, that God laid out kashruit to Noah, since Genesis 7:2 speaks of "clean" and "unclean" animals. Note that there were seven pairs of clean animals brought on board versus *one* pair of the unclean. The reason for this is evident: first, the clean animals were acceptable for use as sacrifice. (Note also that when Noah made landfall, he offered a burnt offering sacrifice of every clean animal and bird (Genesis 8:20). The second reason may be due to the fact that since man was now permitted to eat meat (Genesis 9:3,4), having more "clean" animals than "unclean" allowed the clean to be used for food, since having more of them would increase the "clean" population faster and thus replenish the human food supply.

If nothing else, the point can be argued that from the beginning of Torah up until the time of Yeshua, there was no question as to what was or was not to be eaten. Nowhere over 2,000 years do we find a contradiction of that understanding.

Now, as we come to what we call the "New Testament," suddenly people start coming to the conclusion that since it is the "New" Testament the "Old" one is done away, and we have a "New" set of rules go by — what was not allowed in the older one is now allowed in the new. We now infer that Yeshua pronounced all "foods" clean (Mark 7: 19). We have Kefa getting a vision pronouncing unkosher things as "clean" (Acts 10: 11 - 16) and eating unkosher foods with Gentiles (Galatians 2:11-14). And, we have Sha'ul saying, **"Don't let any one act as your judge with respect to food or drink"** (Colossians 2:16). So, anything goes, folks.

Yet, for a God who doesn't change (James 1: 17; Malachi 3:6; Hebrews 13:8), we certainly see an inconsistency here, especially considering that Yeshua said:

Do not think that I came to abolish the Law or the Prophets; I did not come to abolish, but to fulfill. For truly I say to you, until heaven and earth pass away, not the smallest letter or stroke shall pass away from the law, until all is accomplished. Whoever then annuls one of the least of these commandments, and so teaches others, shall be cared least in the kingdom of heaven; but whoever keeps and teaches them, he shall be called great in the kingdom of heaven (Matthew 5:17-19).

Is God having trouble making up His mind as to what exactly is to be done in this "New Testament," or are some people misinterpreting what's going on here? Certainly not the former.

As mentioned earlier in this book, the only problem with the "Old" covenant was that the people did not keep it (Hebrews 8:6-8; Jeremiah 31: 31-32). It was not that the Laws were bad, unrighteous, or unholy (Romans 7:12); Nor was it that God couldn't get it right the first time and figured His Laws were a little too lofty for His people to reach (Deuteronomy 30:8-14).

No, the problem is plain and simple: we are naturally rebellious to God's commandments since they are external to us and not a part of our nature. The remedy is also simple. When God internalizes the Law within His believers, he or she follows His commandments naturally (Ezekiel 11:17-20; 36:24- 27; 2 Corinthians 3:3-18). That being the case, the Biblical kashruit Laws are still applicable in the New Testament, all the more so because the Law is placed within the believer.

"But, Bruce, we're not 'under the Law.'"

My response: "True, exactly!" How can we be "under" something that is within us? We can't. With the Law being written inside us so that we empowered to keep it, we should obey, not for salvation or justification before God, rather because of our love for God (1 John 5:2,3). We show what kind of believer we are in how, and more importantly why, we keep God's commandments.

With this in mind, how can we reconcile the New Testament passages with the Law as laid out in the Old Testament? First, remember that we are dealing with a Hebrew and not a Greek book in the Bible. We have got to take off our Greek "glasses" (world-view) and put on a new set (actually the original set) of "glasses," the Hebrew one.

The Hebrew viewpoint of "food" is *that which God allowed to be eaten in the Torah,* as previously mentioned. Anything outside of the category of what is to be eaten isn't even called "food!" Lobster, shrimp, pork, clams, crabs, oysters, bear, etc. are not "foods" in the Hebrew viewpoint, so no observant Jew in his or her right mind would have even *thought* to call them by such terminology in Yeshuas' time.

So, when Yeshua in Mark 7:19 declares all "foods" clean, He wasn't declaring that what was "unclean" per Torah was now "clean." Rather, in the context of this passage He was saying that eating with ceremonially washed hands does not cleanse what God has already declared to be clean (i.e. "food").

Sha'ul, in Romans 14, is saying the same thing when he speaks of "food" being clean (verses 14,15, 20). Colossians 2:16 isn't condoning the eating of unclean things, rather that of the clean, since it too was being called "food.." [It should be stressed here that whenever an observant Jew speaks of "food" (and Yeshua, Kefa, Sha'ul, and the early believers were all observant Jews), they are not, I repeat NOT) speaking of anything unkosher Biblically. This was true two-thousand years ago, and it is still true today!]

"Well, what about Kefa's vision," I am asked? Simply this: *let Scripture interpret Scripture.* If an *interpretation* is given, don't go looking for other meanings. When Joseph in Egypt gave the interpretation of their dreams to the chief cupbearer and the chief baker (Genesis 40), should we seek another interpretation? When he interpreted pharaoh's dream in Genesis 41, should we seek another meaning? Or when Daniel interpreted Nebuchadnezzar's dream (Daniel 2), should we spiritualize the interpretation and come up with another that suits us better? To all these, when the Scripture gives a clear interpretation shouldn't we be willing to accept the interpretation? Why can't we do this with Kefa's vision?

Let's place ourselves back in Kefa's time and mentality. You'll note, long after the resurrection of Yeshua (about 10 years), Kefa was still observing a Biblical kashruit (Acts 10: 14). Why? You'd think that if Yeshua was truly proclaiming unclean things as clean back in Mark, he would have already been eating bats, vultures, monkeys, and pork. Yet he remains consistent with Jewish thought and does not eat unclean things.

Now, after the vision, he is perplexed. Is God telling him to do that which he was forbidden in the Law, or was there some other meaning to the vision? Looking back into the context of the passage, it must be remembered that in the time of Yeshua, Gentiles were considered "unclean." [You'll recall that during the judgement of Yeshua by Pilate, Pilate had to come out of his residence to try Him (John 18:28). This was because in that time, to enter into a Gentile house, or touch a Gentile or his possession would mean that the Jew would become ceremonially unclean. An observant Jew would not walk with a Gentile in most circumstances for the same reason.].

Just as the vision is concluded and Kefa is reflecting upon these words, a knock occurs downstairs and three men ask for Kefa.

The Holy Spirit says, **"But arise, go downstairs, and accompany them without misgivings; for I have sent them Myself"** (Acts 10:20). So, Kefa then goes with them:

After arriving at Cornelius' house, Kefa speaks to the people assembled the message of salvation and explains the meaning of the vision to them:

> **"You yourselves know how unlawful it is for a man who is a Jew to associate with a foreigner or to visit him; and yet God has shown me that I should not call any man unholy or unclean. That is why I came without even raising an objection when I was sent for..."** (Acts 10:28,29).

The whole issue (and the only issue) here in Acts 10 and Acts 11: 1-18, as related by Kefa, had nothing to do with eating unclean things. The context deals solely with Gentile believers being part of the covenant community of faith in Yeshua. In Jewish tradition, being a part of the covenant community meant there was to be table relations with the other people within the community. If you have noticed something about most of the Jewish observances, food is almost always considered a part of that observance.

People outside of that covenant community were considered "cut off" from the community, unable to participate in table relations. Therefore, when Gentile believers were brought into the covenant community, a groundwork was laid as to how they were to be brought into the table relationship with the Jewish believers. At the bare minimum, they were to observe the prohibition against the eating of blood so that the Jewish believers would eat with them.

The issue of table relationship (not of unkosher food) is the cause of the incident which Sha'ul cites in Galatians 2:11-21. It was not that Kefa was eating unkosher food with the Gentiles, as many assume. Rather, that he was eating with Gentiles (verse 12) when the party of the circumcision (Jewish believers) were not present, yet he would hold himself aloof from the

Gentiles when they came (verse 12). It seems that Kefa was still struggling with the traditional issue of the Gentiles and their being unclean. When in the presence of his fellow Jews, he would be stand offish from the Gentile believers, and when they were gone, he was willing to eat with them, thus being hypocritical. This is why Sha'ul was confronting him.

Finally, there is the issue of Acts 15, relative to the Gentiles. If *all* a Gentile had to do when coming to faith in Yeshua was to follow these passages, then he or she must at least abstain from eating blood (verses 20, 29) following the Old Testament Noachide prohibition against the ingesting of blood (Genesis 9:4), or things offered to idols.

Once saved, however, since Moses is preached in the synagogues every Sabbath, a Gentile would come to know that there is more to being holy than the Noachide Laws, and, presumably would, out of love for God, begin to follow them.

The whole issue of Biblical kashruit, as far as God is concerned, is that of holiness. When we look at Leviticus 11, we see God concluding this chapter with:

> **For I am the Lord your God. Consecrate yourselves therefore, and be holy; for I am holy. And you shall not make yourselves unclean with any of the swarming things that swarm on the earth For I am the Lord, who brought you up from the land of Egypt, to be your God; thus you shall be holy for I am holy. This is the law regarding the animal and the bird, and every living thing that moves in the waters, and every thing that swarms on the earth, to make a distinction between the unclean and the clean, and between the edible creature and the creature which is not to be eaten (verses 44-47).**

The obvious question is: What *does eating* have to do with God's holiness anyway? Since God does not eat, why does God place this passage as a conclusion as to what one may or may not eat?

I believe that God is speaking about a spiritual issue here, since He is Spirit (John 4:24). I believe that when He defines something as unclean, it is *spiritually unclean* and when one eats something unclean, he or she becomes spiritually unclean, spiritually defiled. The issue isn't about food — processing, refrigeration or cooking – it is solely about spiritual holiness. I believe that there is no one in a better position than God to know what is clean and what is unclean, since He is omniscient!

How does what we eat defile us or make us unholy? Let me illustrate this with an example that is easier to relate to. Let me ask you a question: "How does having sexual intercourse with another person (other than our spouse) defile us?"

Is it because there is something physically unclean about sexual intercourse? Physically speaking, there is no difference between the genitals of one man over another man, or one woman over another woman. Functionally, in sexual intercourse, the procedure is the same between one heterosexual couple and another. So, what *is* defiling about a heterosexual man having sexual intercourse with someone other than his wife? Is it physically or spiritually defiling? Of course, it is easy to see that it is spiritually defiling. I am sure the simplest person can answer that question, so I shouldn't have to spell it out further.

In the same way, what is so defiling about eating unclean meat? Is it the meat itself? Is there something physically wrong with the meat? Often, there is. Pork is loaded with fat and worm eggs; proper cooking will kill the larvae; proper refrigeration will keep it from spoiling. Yet, assuming we prepare it correctly, will it become clean? Physically, that may happen. You may get every worm egg and every bit of fat out, but if we're talking about spiritual uncleanness here, proper preparation will not change its status. It is still unclean.

Let me ask another obvious question. "'Physically, if I wore a condom, prepared properly, and then asked God to bless the act; - is it ok for me to have sex with someone other than my wife?" I hope you can answer that one. Of course not! In summary, you may prepare and prepare, but if God declares something is defiling or unclean, it doesn't change it in the spiritual realm. If it's unclean, it's unclean! Why is it so simple to see in the example of sex, yet so difficult when it relates to eating? When God says by eating them**"Do not render yourselves detestable,** (Leviticus 11: 41-43) the resulting **spiritual** defilation is exactly the **same** Hebrew word as the defilation caused by a male having sex with another male, or someone having sex with an animal (Leviticus 18:22).

Let's take a look at this from the Hebrew:

In Leviticus 11:4 the Scripture states:

> **Only, you may not eat these, of those bringing up the cud, and of those dividing the hoof: the camel, though it brings up the cud, yet it does not divide the hoof, it is unclean** (Hebrew: "taw-may").

The meaning of "taw-may" can be seen when look it up in Strongs Hebrew & Chaldee Dictionary— number **2930,** meaning **"to be foul especially in a ceremonial or moral sense (contaminated): defile (self), pollute (self), be (make, make self, pronounce) unclean X (multiplied utterly)."**[16]

This same word is used many times to describe unclean things throughout the Older Testament, but rather than going through each and every passage with you, I shall highlight two here to make my point. Leviticus 18:22-24 states:

> **And you shall not lie with a male as one lies with a woman; it is detestable. And with any animal, you shall not give your lying down with it for uncleanness (2930) with it. And a woman shall not stand before an animal,**

---

16 *A CONCISE DICTIONARY of the words in THE HEBREW BIBLE with their renderings in the AUTHORIZED ENGLISH VERSION,* by James Strong, S.T.D., L.L.D., MACDONALD PUBLISHING COMPANY, McLean, VA, page 46

to lie with it; it is a shameful thing. Do not defile (2930) yourself with all these, for with all these the nations have been defiled (2930) , which I expelling before you and the land is defiled (2930) and I will visit its iniquity on it.

In other words, by eating these unclean things, a person makes him or herself just as spiritually defiled as if he or she were having sex with someone of the same sex or having sex with an animal. (Sort of changes the perspective of things, doesn't it?)

Contextually speaking, if you want to make yourself abominable in the spiritual realm, have sex with a person not your spouse, or with someone of your own sex, or with an animal, or go have a ham sandwich. The resultant defilation is all the same according to God's definition.

Lest you believe that I have taken it of context, I will conclude this chapter with the second passage found in Leviticus 20:25-26:

And you shall make a difference between the clean animal the unclean (2931), and between the unclean (2931) fowl and the clean. And you shall not defile your souls (spiritual defilement, friends) by beast or by fowl, or by anything which swarms the ground, which I have set apart to you as unclean (2930) - and you shall be holy to Me, for I, Jehovah, am holy; and I have set you apart from the nations to become Mine. [17] (A LITERAL TRANSLATION OF THE BIBLE)

God says that He wants us to be a holy people, as He is holy. A believer's desire should be to be holy as God is holy. God alone knows how we are to do this, and if we read His Word and obey it we will learn how to be holy. This is as true in the realm of sex as it is in anything else; including what we eat.

---

17 *A LITERAL TRANSLATION OF THE BIBLE*, Copyright 1985, by Jay P. Green, Sr.

Just as a believer in Yeshua is commanded not to take away the members of Messiah and make them members of a harlot (1 Corinthians 6:15-20) because they will literally be making the Messiah a partaker of their sin with them, so I believe a believer should avoid all unclean or unholy contact - even with things we eat. As believers, our bodies no longer belong to us, but to Him; for we have been purchased with a price and are His temple. So then, we literally have to bring our appetites under His control and not simply yielding to our own pleasures.

As a result, if we defile the temple with unclean or unholy things or behavior, we are corrupting that which Messiah so dearly paid for: our bodies. The question is: are we truly His? Does He truly own us? Or does He only own the parts of us we allow Him to?

Perhaps He owns us on our day of worship and not the rest of the week. Perhaps He owns us in whatever money we choose to give, but not in our tithe, or in the other areas of our finances.Perhaps He owns us in our area of sexuality and not in what we eat. Perhaps He owns very little of our lives. We need to seriously evaluate what we are giving up to His ownership in our lives and then see if we are truly His. We may find that He owns very little of what He paid so dearly for...

Chapter 10
How'd we Ever Get This Way?

The first believers in Yeshua after His resurrection were either Jewish or full proselytes (Acts 2:10).It was **not** until roughly 10 years *after* Pentecost that the first non-proselytic gentile (Cornelius-Acts 10) came into the faith. And, not until the middle of the second century, that the "church," as it has come to be known, became a predominantly Gentile body.

Up until that time, all early Christian theology was Jewish: and the concepts it used were quarried chiefly from the Old Testament. The believers in Yeshua were not considered to be outside the stream of Judaism, but rather another sect of Judaism called **"the Nazarines"** (Acts 24:5-15).

"Devout" (Acts 22:12) and **"zealous for the Law"** (Acts 21:20), these early believers kept the seventh-day Sabbath (Acts 13:14,44; 16:13;17:1,2; 18:4), observed Shavuot (Pentecost-Act 2:1; 20:16), Yom Kippur (Acts 27:9) , the Feast of Unleavened Bread (Acts 12:3- 20:6), and worshiped in the Temple and synagogues (Acts 2:46, 3:1-3; 5:20-25; 9:20; 13:14, 43; 14:1; 17: l,2; 18:4-8; 19:8).

As mentioned earlier, the Apostle Sha'ul even offered the sacrifice of the Nazirite (Numbers 6) in the Temple (Acts 21:23-26) many, many **years** after the resurrection of Yeshua. In effect, what we are seeing is a Torah-abiding group of believers, led by a believing, Jewish leadership of that day. Today, we basically have a non-Torah-abiding group of believers, led by believing Gentile leadership in the context non-Jewish Christianity, having little or no resemblance to the practice of first century "Christianity." In essence, the Christianity that came into the "church" from the paganistic practices of the Gentiles, is foreign to that of the Apostle's practice.

Most Christians are totally unaware of how anti-Law, paganistic attitude crept into the Body of Messiah. In fact, most believers think that the faith they practice is the very one of the first century believing community of Messiah. They believe that the Apostles celebrated Yeshuas' birthday, and that they celebrated Easter (oops!) "Resurrection Day."

They didn't. And, if today's pastors and/or teachers are aware of this, either they think it irrelevant, or they are afraid that they'll lose their following if they "rock the boat."

Yet, God, in His word, *expressly* forbids His people forbids His people from following the paganistic customs of the nations! Many in the Body of Messiah are quick to point out how Israel fell into paganism throughout the Old Testament writings, but are blind to the paganistic practices in today's Body of Messiah.

We often continue to practice these customs because they have become the standard in our churches.

We accept these practices as if they were instituted from God without realizing that when we do the same, we're as guilty as the Pharisees in Matthew 15, whose traditions invalidated God's commandments. As an example, in the church Christmas is observed (which God in no way commanded) and the Feast of Weeks (Pentecost-which God did command) is neglected. Easter is celebrated and Pesach (Passover) is neglected. The Sabbath is observed on the first day of the week and not on the specified seventh day.

"But Jesus fulfilled these feasts, so we don't have to keep them."

Tell that to the Disciples, who kept the faithfully, as already noted earlier in this chapter. Tell that to the early believing community who observed them faithfully until Constantine gained control of it.In fact, the early believing community observed

Passover until the Council of Nicea (325 A.D.).Daniel Gruber in his book, *THE CHURCH AND THE JEW - The Biblical Relationship,* notes:

> **Jesus had celebrated Passover on the fourteenth day of Nisan because that is its Biblical date. He observed all the Levitical holy days on the days when God had decreed and designed them to be observed. The Apostles and the First century Church did much the same.**

> **At first, the Christian Passover was celebrated at the same time as the Jewish. This simultaneous observance was preserving the Jewish ritual in the Christian festival and strengthening the bonds between Christianity and Judaism. The date must be changed. In some quarters the Church attempted to restrict the cerebration to a single day — 14 Nisan and this became the prevailing custom-she made Holy Week the week in which fell 14 Nisan (the day when the Jewish feast began), and removed the festival, which had already changed its character, to the Sunday following Holy Week In all these cases there was a dependence on the Jewish calendar, a humiliating subjection to the Synagogue which irked the Church .....**

> **The issue... was finally settled by the Council of Nicea in 325 A.D. There it was decided that all the churches should celebrate the Passover, or actually Easter, on the ecclesiastically chosen Sunday rather than the Biblical date. All the churches were thus informed. The Emperor Constantine sent his personal exhortation to all the churches concerning the decision of the Council .....**

> **In this letter, Constantine officially establishes an anti-Judaic foundation for the doctrine and practice of the Church, and declares that contempt for the Jews and**

separation from them is the only proper Christian attitude."[18]

Daniel Gruber articulates another important question that should be weighed carefully by every believer in own practice of the faith goes. "When did God give such authority over the Church to Constantine?"

It was Constantine who decreed that the Sabbath be changed from the seventh day to the first day of the week, **not the Apostles**. The Christian Sunday was not made a "day of rest" until Constantine decreed it so in A.D. 321, when he called it.- **"the venerable day of the Sun (Sunday)."**[19]

Why did he do this? He did it because his previous religion was the worship of the "Unconquered Sun." Retaining the pagan symbols was a necessary compromise with his pagan subjects, still very much in the majority.

The Christian church took over many pagan ideas and images. From sun-worship, for example, came the celebration of Christ's birth on the twenty-fifth of December, the birthday of the Sun. Saturnalia, the Roman winter festival of 17-21 December, provided the merriment, gift-giving and candles typical of later Christmas holidays.[20]

The First mention of Christmas as a festival of the church on 25 December, refers to A.D. 336. It comes in the Philocalian Catalogue (354), a civil and religious calendar compiled at Rome. In the East, 6 January, known as Epiphany, was favoured as the anniversary of Christ's

---

18 *THE CHURCH AND THE JEWS, The Biblical Relationship*, pages 25-31 78

19 *EERDMAN'S HANDBOOK TO THE HISTORY OF CHRISTIANITY,* Copyright 1977, WM. B. EERDMAN'S PUBLISHING CO., Grand Rapids, MI., pages 122- 131

20 *IBID.*, page 131

birth and baptism. The Western date was introduced into the East by John Chrysostom near the end of the fourth century.

Subsequently the birth of Christ was celebrated by both East and West on 25 December.[21]

By 600 A.D. the believing community had acquired virtually all the paganistic practices that it was to incorporate from many of the religions practiced in the Roman Empire. Through compromise, the Believing community had adopted as tradition that which was forbidden to the Jewish people.

It must be remembered that the Jewish people were to destroy the peoples, in the land they were coming into so that they would not compromise the standards God had given them. Yet, they did not, and so fell into the paganistic practices of the people they were to conquer, just as God warned.

It is so easy to follow after the practices of the world, which practices are anti-God and anti-holy.

God knew this. That is why those anti-God, anti-holy people were to be destroyed, so God's people would not be corrupted.

Will God excuse the believing community for following the paganistic practices of the nations it embraced when He did not excuse His chosen people? I think not.

I think as believers we need to be true to God and ourselves. How much paganism in our faithwalk is acceptable and how much is not? Do Protestants have the right to criticize Catholics for some of their paganistic practices when we have so many of our own?

I wish to exhort believers in every denomination to come out from these pagan practices in all forms and go back to the God-given, Biblically commanded Holy Days and practices. I pray

---

21 *IBID.*, page 147 79

that all believer stop compromising with the world and seek to do God's things in His way. In so doing, we will truly come back to the form of worship and practice found in the First Century believing community.

CHAPTER 11

"Tradition Tradition, Tradition"

So went the song that Reb Tevya sang in the epic movie *FIDDLER ON THE ROOF*.

Yet, a truth rings so strikingly clear in the struggles portrayed by these Orthodox Jews in Czarist Russia that applies not only to the Jewish community depicted in the movie, but also to today's Christian community, as well.

When our cherished traditional ways of looking at life in general, and the Scriptures in particular, are seriously challenged, we feel the most threatened, feeling the vertigo from having the "rug pulled out from under our feet."

Never mind that the challenge which comes against our tradition is pure, unadulterated truth, we'll fight against it tooth and nail and stubbornly hang on to our traditions. Yet, that is exactly the issue that Yeshua, Truth Incarnate (John 14:6) was dealing with in His discourse with the Pharisees.

Once, when He was criticized by them because His disciples violated the traditions of the elders by not ceremonially washing their hands when they ate bread, He responded to the Pharisees:

"And why do you yourselves transgress the commandment of God for the sake of your tradition?" (Matthew 15:3)

We in the Body of Messiah are so quick to point an accusing finger at the Pharisees for their apparent hypocrisy, yet we do not see the same log in our own eyes when we do the same things. The traditions of the Pharisees of Yeshuas' day didn't just pop out of nowhere, they were the result of centuries of accumulation of thought and practice. Most of the time, these practices went on unquestioned with son emulating father, daughter emulating mother, generation after generation, until it reached its current state — that is, until some iconoclast comes along (like Yeshua or the Prophets) and upsets the table, so to speak.

It calls to mind a story I once heard: A mother was teaching her young daughter how to cook roast one day and as she prepared to place the meat into the large cooking pan, she took a large knife and lopped off the top and bottom portions of the meat.

"Mommy," the daughter asked, "Why did you just cut off the top and bottom of the roast?" After thinking about it for a moment, the mother replied, "You know, it's a family tradition, I really don't know. I just remember your grandma doing that when she cooked roast. Let's call Grandma and find out."

When Grandma picked up the phone, the mother asked, "Mom, why is it when you made roast that you cut off the top and bottom pieces of meat?"

Grandma answered, "I cut off the top and bottom pieces because my cooking pans were not large enough to hold the whole piece, so I cut it down to fit."

It is the same way with our traditions (and the Pharisees, too, I might add). What perhaps started off as a practical way of doing something became an unquestioned, almost sacred, way of doing things.No doubt in the Pharisees' ceremonial washing, when they ate bread, or in their other traditions, a practical reason necessitated what eventually became "tradition." Yet, by the time it reached those whom Yeshua criticized, what had started as a practical means of doing something spiritual became equated with Law —something that had to be done without question.

I think that over time the Pharisees have gotten a bad rap by the believing community. In reality, I do not think they were any different than most of us. To give them the benefit of the doubt, I really believe that they were sincere about their belief. I am certain they didn't regard themselves as hypocrites! I think they thought they were doing exactly what God wanted them to do. They took what they were taught and observed their practices as though it were from God.

Yet are they any different than most of us in our religious practice? Think about it: do we question why we say a blessing before we eat a meal? I know people who don't pray to God at any other time of the day, except for these four times: before each of their three meals and at bedtime. When asked why, they reply that those were the times they prayed when they were children.

"What is so wrong with that?" I am asked.

Nothing, so long as that tradition does not violate God's commandments. Many times traditions, in and themselves, are neither good nor evil; it's what we do with them that matters.

Yeshuas' response to the Pharisees gets to the heart of this matter. When our traditions cause us neglect or violate a direct commandment of God, they are wrong and must either discontinued or relegated to a secondary place beneath the commandment. In other words, do commandment first, and then if you have time (and if it doesn't violate God's commandment) do the tradition.

Let me give an example: God in His Word commanded that certain days are to be regarded as Holy and are to be perpetually observed. When a tradition, like Christmas, is celebrated *instead of* this Holy Day, God's Word is *invalidated* because the tradition took precedence over the commandment.If one must observe Christmas, then the Holy Days are not to be neglected. Observe the Holy Days first, and if you have time for Christmas go ahead and observe it! (Not that I'm recommending believers observe this pagan practice at all; I am simply making a point).

In the Jewish tradition, Channukah is observed. It is not a Biblically commanded observance at all.

Yet, Yeshua observed it in John 10:22.

However, He also observed all of God's *commanded* Days; He did not place a tradition over commandment! Incidentally, God does no necessarily want us to give up all our traditions, just the one's that violate His commandments or replace a real, heartfelt relationship with Him.

Can we sincerely look at all of the traditions an doctrines of man and see if we aren't doing what we criticize the Pharisees for doing? If we can't, then we are just as guilty as they, and have no ground to throw stones at these men.

This is the challenge we are faced with today, and it is no less difficult today than it was 2000 years ago. In fact, I daresay it will be more difficult, given that we have an additional millennia of accumulated traditions over what they had.

Yet, if we want to arrive at the truth, we need to see beyond our sacred cows of tradition and human doctrine and compare it to the Word of God. If it stands up to the test, keep it; if not, chuck it.

Just as the Bereans in Act 17:11 tested the teachings of Sha'ul **"to see whether these things were so,"** we must test all things, **"holding fast to what is good and abstaining from every form of evil"** (1 Thessalonians 5:21). The mark of a true believer in God is a hunger for God's truth and an uncompromising zeal to hold on to it once found.

There are many, such as the Pharisees, who thought they had found God's truth in their traditions and practices, and were unwilling (or unable) to change even when confronted by the real truth. They are like Reb Tevya, who, when challenged, got angry when his traditions were questioned.

I believe it is high time for the true believers in Yeshua to challenge and question what has been taught and seek truth - no matter what the cost. We must be mature and brave enough as believers to be *willing* to put aside all practices that are weighed in the balance and found wanting. To do any less will subject us to the same criticism as Yeshua gave the Pharisees:

"You hypocrites, rightly did Isaiah prophesy of you, saying, 'This people honors Me with their lips, but their heart is far away from Me. But in vain do they worship Me, teaching as doctrines the precepts of men'" (Matthew 15:7-8).

If we are truly "People of the Book," perhaps we ought to go back to "the Book" to establish our practices. If the writings of the New Testament can't be used to justify our disregard of the commandments of God, why don't we just quit our anti-Scriptural practices and go back to keeping God's commandments? When we do that, we will truly be living what we are believing.

The bottom line is this: Are we willing to pay the price necessary to stand for truth? The power to decide lies with us alone, and the power to stand lies in the power of God. Nobody can decide for us; we must do it ourselves. But, whatever we decide, we must answer someday before God. At that time, we won't be able to point our finger at our pastor, priest, elder, deacon, teacher and say that it was his or her fault we practiced as we did for the truth was found within the Word of God for all to see.

Lest someone say, **"'There is no condemnation for those who are in Christ Jesus** (Romans 8:1),' and you are condemning the church."

I wish to respond to that by saying that I am not condemning the church. Remember, the Scriptures are *also* for reproof (1 Timothy 3:16), and what I am doing is just that. It may sound harsh, but as surgery is necessary and painful to remove the cancerous tumor, so reproof must be as sharp in order to remove the uncleanliness from among us.

I believe what Yeshua said in Matthew 5:19 with regard to the commandments is true. Believers who **"keep and teach them"** will be called great in the kingdom of heaven; those believers who annul (and teach others to annul) the least of the commandments are still saved (in the kingdom of heaven) and are not condemned but risk being called **"least in the kingdom of heaven"** for doing so. [Yeshua didn't even mention those who break important commandments (e.g., the TEN COMMAND-MENTS, including the seventh-day Sabbath].

In the Book of Hosea (4:6) God says,

"My people are destroyed for a lack of knowledge. Because you have rejected knowledge, I also will reject you from being priests for Me, because you have forgotten the Law of your God, I will also forget your children."

Notice the second phrase of this passage, **"because you have rejected knowledge..."** It does not say that you are destroyed because you did not know, you did not hear, or you were not taught, rather, it states that you are destroyed because you willingly chose to reject the knowledge before you. Anyone with a Bible has the means of knowing God and learning about His wisdom and plans for their life. It is a matter of heart; if we are willing to truly know Him and His ways through study, we will find Him by seeking Him.

To all who have ears to hear, let them hear. Please repent of your pagan practices and come back to God's commandments. Don't let tradition keep you from the blessings of being a part of the kingdom of God.

Chapter 12

WWJD? What Would Jesus (Yeshua) Do?

Over the last several years, a popular item among Christian children (and some adults, I might add) has been a wrist band with the initials "WWJD?" This acronym stands for the words, "What Would Jesus Do?"

While I am not being critical of the practice of wearing things like these to remind us to live holy lives (in fact, I welcome anything that leads us to such thinking), I think that people who promote the wearing of these items sometimes often fail to realize the scope of what they are saying.

It must be remembered that Yeshua was totally obedient to the commandments as pertained to an Israelite (a citizen of Israel). As believers in him, we are all made part of that same commonwealth (Ephesians 2:11-22) whether we are Jew or non-Jew. Because of this, all the laws of this community apply to all within the community. The sojourner follows the same laws as the native. There are no separate laws for Jews and another set of laws for non-Jews; we are all one.

Since Yeshua showed us by his life how an Israelite is to live, the acronym "WWJD" is quite appropriate. When confronted by various situations in life, we should ask "WWJD?" What Would Yeshua Do? Would he succumb to lust? Would he go ahead and have sexual intercourse with a woman not his spouse? Would he even lust after her, even though he did not carry it to its eventual end with intercourse?

If we didn't know the answer, where would we turn to obtain it? Of course, we would go to the Bible. Would Yeshua lust for her? No! He says in the book of Matthew:

You have heard that it was said, "You shall not commit adultery"; but I say to you, that everyone who looks on a woman to lust for her has committed adultery with her already in his heart (Chapter 5, verses 27, 28).

The answer to the question is found clearly. Not only would he not commit adultery with her, but he wouldn't even lust for her. Yeshua goes to the heart of the matter; adultery is preceded by lust.If you wish to avoid committing adultery, avoid lusting after someone.

Having now found the answer in Scripture, the person wearing the "WWJD?" band implies that they will follow what he would have done in the same situation.

Now, I realize that we will all fall short of what Yeshua would have done (that is what sin is) and won't always do what he did. Yet, having said that, we often excuse ourselves in our sin by saying, "I'm just human..." or, as the saying that was popularized by Flip Wilson goes, "The Devil made me do it..." and we go on sinning anyway as if we have no other choice.

Well, Scripture says there is another choice: the choice to do good; the choice to do what he did.This choice is the choice to be free from the bondage of sin. There was a time in our lives before we became believers in him that we had no choice. We were in bondage to sin (Romans 6) and sin reigned over us, but now we are freed from sin (verse 18). We have a choice to do as Yeshua did!

When we ask the question "WWJD?" we are saying that our choice is to do what he wants us to do; what he would have done himself in the same situation. What we need to do is to broaden the question to see if there are areas in our lives that do not live up to "WWJD?"

It is fairly simple to answer the question "WWJD?" in the area of sexual promiscuousness, or stealing, or lying, or worshiping false gods. We will have a lot of other believers bringing us to those Scriptures if we practice these things. Yet, there are many things that Yeshua would not have done that most believers do without even raising the question "WWJD?

For instance, would Yeshua eat pork, or shellfish, or any unkosher thing? "WWJD?" Would Yeshua celebrate the pagan practices of the Caananites or other peoples surrounding Israel? "WWJD?" What day of the week would Yeshua observe as the Sabbath (day of rest)? "WWJD?" Would Yeshua compromise his holy living when other people weren't looking? "WWJD?"

When we consider the implications of the question "WWJD?" we find that it is greater and deeper than we first realized. The question goes to the essence of what he was ans is: holy. The answer to the question speaks to us and says:

> **the one who says he abides in him ought to walk in the same manner as he walked** (1 John 2:6)

When we say that we are believers in him, we are saying that we will walk as he walked. Not only must we walk his walk in the more obvious ways, but we must learn to walk his walk in those less obvious ways that are just as important to holy living. If we don't, we are making the Messiah a partaker in our sin.

When we became believers in the Lord, we became one spirit with him. Our body members became members of the Messiah and his Holy Spirit dwells in us.

> **Do you not know that your bodies are members of Messiah? Shall I then take away the members of Messiah and make them members of a harlot? May it never be!**

Or do you not know that your body is a temple of the Holy Spirit who is in you, whom you have from God, and that you are not your own? For you have been bought with a price: therefore glorify God in your body. (1 Corinthians 6:15,19)

When we sin, he is in us; he is partaking with us: We are defiling his temple. I am sure he doesn't like that, though he realizes as believers we will sin from time-to-time. We often ignorantly sin because we don't know the Scriptures as we ought or were mis-told.

Sometimes, we do it deliberately; even though we know what the Scripture says. But when we truly repent of our sin (turn around from our sins), ask forgiveness for our sin and choose to do what is right, God will forgive us and heal us.

Since he dwells in us, the Lord expects us to live holy lives. We should care what we do with him living inside of us. We should ask the question "WWJD?" and search the Scriptures diligently to find the answer. To do that, we must put human tradition and doctrine aside in favor of the Scripture's position and seek to walk as he walked.

Chapter 13

Where Do we Go From Here?

When all is said and done, it is up to the individual to choose what to do when presented with the facts. Perhaps it will be decided that he or she will continue on with their current practice, unaffected.Perhaps it will be that there will be a complete renunciation of pagan practices in their life.

Regardless, we will all have to account before God for what we did with the light we were given.For those who decide to do nothing, you will not have to go any farther in this book; it will not make a difference in your life anyway.

For those who decide to make partial or complete changes in their relationship expression of their faith in Yeshua, I will attempt to help you get some direction of possible things that can be done. I will assume that the reader wishes to make a complete change in their practice of faith, which will require a necessary change in lifestyle.

Anyone wishing to stop short of any of these suggestions may do so, remembering that it is not me they have to answer to, but the Lord. With that in mind, here are some things which may guide you:

1. Stop observing the "obvious" pagan practices found within the Body of Messiah. Those practices incorporated into the Body of Messiah from very early on with pagan origins have no place in the Body of Messiah: Christmas, Easter, Lent, Good Friday, Halloween (or All Saint's Day), and the Sunday "sabbath" are all pagan in orientation and origin. They subvert the purity of the faith and contaminate its practitioners. [Once again, I would like to reiterate that one may worship ANY DAY, for in the Temple, worship occurred EVERY DAY. You may worship on Sunday, or Monday, or whatever day you choose, but Sabbath means "rest", and one is to REST on the SEV-ENTH day of the week.]

2. Begin to observe the clearly Biblical commandments that can be seen in the Scripture such as: observing the Biblical kosher laws, not committing forbidden sexual practices, not eating blood, and regarding the period of time from Friday evening to Saturday evening as the true Sabbath in which work is not to be performed, as clearly specified. Then, as you read the Word, the Holy Spirit will bring to your attention other commandments and will show you sin in other areas of your life. As He does so, understand that He does this for your benefit and blessing.

3. Begin to learn how to observe the Biblical feasts and Holy Days and begin to incorporate them into your life to replace all the pagan traditions. You can do this by preferably visiting a Messianic Jewish synagogue, because of their belief in Yeshua as the Messiah. If one is not available, call a local rabbi and find out how they're celebrated. Perhaps they may let you observe their practice and you can go from there. (Remember, they may be observing these out of a legalistic perspective in keeping the Law. The Law is NOT to be kept this way, rather, out of love for the Lord.) May I suggest reading Messianic Jewish books on God's appointed feast days and times to help you?

4. Begin to learn about the Jewishness of the faith and go back to the Jewishness of the First Century believing community. If believers don't insist upon this, their Pastors will continue the pagan traditions of the believing community; it is so much easier to "keep on doing things as usual." "Tradition, Tradition, TRADITION!" (So the song goes...).

5. I would encourage you to try NOT to leave your church in any event. Instead, if possible, act as a catalyst of change to cause fellow believers to give up their pagan practices and return to a Biblical observance. If, however, that can't be accomplished in your local denomination, then leave.

Expect persecution from fellow believers. The believing community is the only group that seems to kick, beat or shoot its wounded and hurting. Those who have lived righteously have always been misunderstood, stoned, or otherwise maligned for doing what God wanted them to do. 2 Timothy 3:12 speaks to the fact that all who desire to live godly lives will be persecuted. Sadly, it too often comes from our brethren in the faith. Stand firm and hang in there! Don't give up on what the Bible says to do to show your love for God. You'll probably not receive a pat on the back for keeping Biblical kosher; instead, you'll find other Christians deliberately setting traps for you to break it. Don't be surprised; this has happened to me and many others at times. When all is said and done, it is better to err on what the Word says than what man-made traditions say. They won't be standing there along side you when you are accounting for your deeds before Almighty God.

Finally, begin to use the spiritual gifts as outlined in Romans 12; 1 Corinthians 12; Ephesians 4:11-16. I believe these gifts will become much more pronounced and effective once the garbage of paganism is removed from your life. As we truly become more holy (separate) from the worldly practices, we will be more of an unclogged conduit for God's power to flow through. I believe the final Revival will be marked by a great outpouring of God's power that was not equaled, even by the early Believing community.

The most important question to ask at this point is: "Do we want to be used by God this way? If not, we can continue just as before and let Egypt, Babylon, Greece, and Rome rule our religious practices. We're comfortable with these traditions; they've been around a long, long time; and we're doing okay (so we think).

On the other hand, if we choose to get our lives cleaned up, and we, as the "Bride making herself ready for the Bridegroom," go back to the Biblical principles outlined in the whole Bible, we will see God making manifest His love, grace and power in the lives of millions. The choice is not an easy one...choose wisely.

BIBLIOGRAPHY

I. Related to the Older Testament

Brooks, Roger, *The Spirit of the Ten Commandments: Shattering the Myth of Rabbinic Legalism*, San Francisco, CA: Harper & Row, 1990

Dyrness, William, *Themes in Old Testament Theology,* Downers Grove, IL: Inter Varsity Press, 1979

Green, Sr., Jay P., *A LITERAL TRANSLATION OF THE BIBLE*, 1985

Hamilton, Victor P., *HANDBOOK ON PENTATEUCH*, Grand Rapids, MI: Baker Book House, 1982

Hertz , J.H. Editor, *The PENTATEUCH AND HAFTORAHS*, Second Edition, London, England, Soncino Press, 1987

Kaiser, Walter C. Jr., *Toward an Old Testament Theology*, Grand Rapids, MI: Zondervan, 1978

Michael Hilton & Gordian Marshall, *The Gospels & Rabbinic Judaism- A Study Guide,* Hoboken, NJ: KTAV Publishing House, 1988

Neusner, Jacob. *THE FOUNDATIONS OF THE THEOLOGY OF JUDAISM,* Northvale, NJ- Jason Aaronson, Inc., 1991

Schultz, Samuel J., *the Gospel of Moses,* Chicago, IL: Moody Press, 1979

Schultz, Samuel J., *The Old Testament Speaks*, San Francisco, CA: Harper & Row, 1960

Werblowsky, Dr. R.J. Zwi and Wigoder, Dr. Geoffrey *THE ENCYCLOPEDIA OF THE JEWISH RELIGION*, ADAMA BOOKS 1986

II. The Jewish Roots of the Christian Faith

Eckstein, Yechiel, *What Christians Should know About Jews and Judaism*, Waco, TX: Word Publishing, 1984

Juster, Daniel, *Jewish Roots - A Foundation of Biblical Theology*, Rockville, MD: DAVAR Publishing, 1986

Wilson, Marvin, *Our Father Abraham: Jewish Roots of the Christian Faith*, Grand Rapids, MI: Eerdmans Publishing, 1989

III. Related to the Newer Testament

Biven, David & Blizzard, Roy, Jr., *Understanding the difficult words of Jesus*, Shippensberg, PA: Center for Biblical Analysis, 1983

Stern, David H., *Jewish New Testament Commentary*, Clarksville, MD: Jewish New Testament Publications, 1992

IV. Church History

Bacchiocchi, Samuele, *FROM SABBATH TO SUNDAY*, THE PONTIFICAL GREGORIAN UNIVERSITY PRESS, Rome: 1977 *EERDMAN'S HANDBOOK TO THE HISTORY OF CHRISTIANITY*, WM. B. EERDMAN'S PUBLISHING CO.: Grand Rapids, MI:1977

Gruber, Daniel, *THE CHURCH AND THE JEWS, The Biblical Relationship*, GENERAL COUNCIL OF THE ASSEMBLIES OF GOD, Springfield, MO: 1991

Roberts, Alexander & Donaldson, James, *The Ante-Nicene Fathers, Volume 1*, WM. B. EERDMANS PUBLISHING CO., Grand Rapids, MI: 1987

V. Related to Biblical Languages

Cranfield, C.E.B. *THE INTERNATIONAL CRITICAL COMMENTARY, ROMANS*, 1979

Gesenius, H.W.F. *Gesenius ' Hebrew-Chaldee Lexicon to the Old Testament*, BAKER BOOK HOUSE, Grand Rapids, MI:1979

Strong, James S.T.D., L.L.D. , *A CONCISE DICTIONARY of the words in THE HEBREW BIBLE with their renderings in the AUTHORIZED ENGLISH VERSION*, MACDONALD PUBLISHING COMPANY, McLean, VA

Vine, W.E., *Vine's Expository Dictionary of Biblical Words*, THOMAS NELSON PUBLISHERS, New York: 1985

VI. Related to Holy Living

Juster, Dr. Daniel C., *Growing to Maturity A Messianic Jewish Guide*, The Union of Messianic Jewish Congregations Press, Gaithersburg, MD: 1982, 1985, 1987